INTO THE VOID

Nick Power

erbacce-press
Liverpool UK

5 Farrell Close, Melling, Liverpool, L31 1BU, UK

erbacce-press publications Liverpool UK 2018

erbacce-press.com
ISBN: 978-1-907878-97-8

ACKNOWLEDGEMENTS

The Coral (past & present). Aja Frais. Austin Collings. Andrew Taylor & Alan Corkish at erbacce-press. Steven Cherry. James Skelly. Lois Wilson. Jo Kendall. Alan Wills. Kev & Liam Power. Sheila & Steve Power. Alfie Skelly. Conrad & Dave at SJM. John Leahy & all at Ignition. Touring crew (past & present).

INDEX:

CHAPTER ONE

CONNECTOR

A five-year break comes to an end. New album complete.
Rehearsals. Learning to play again. Crime movie themes.
Promotion, interviews, radio sessions. Paris.
A photograph shoot in New Brighton.

BOXING DAY and CHASING THE TAIL

Boxing Day, 2015. The day the first song from our new album, *Distance Inbetween,* is released. It goes online early, around 8am. and I miss the unveiling because I'm sleeping off a hangover in the spare room of my mum's house, where there had been a Christmas party the night before.

I wake up, switch on my phone and see the video all over the internet. People have been trying to ring me all morning. There are voicemails and a backlog of unread messages.

Straight away I feel the butterflies in my gut. The nervous energy. A feeling like you've jumped onto a moving train and you're not sure where it's headed. All you know is it's going fast and it might not stop at all. And wherever it ends up, it'll be an eventful ride.

Anyway, I'm sitting there at the table, thinking maybe I should get my keyboard chops in shape because all I've done for the past six months, besides record the album, is watch movies and read detective comics. Suddenly, I see all of that fall away.

I stand up and look out of the kitchen window. A posse of cats has gathered on the wall that backs into the alleyway. They're just sitting there in the afternoon drizzle, wasting time. It seems to me that in this moment that they're golden, untouchable. They're sending out some message to the other animals in the area. The dogs, the rats, the pigeons. It's clear as day.

I move back up the stairs to throw some clothes on. To get up, to get out, to face the world. It's like I'm awake again.

Hoylake, 26/12/15

GRAVITY'S RAINBOW

In the period between 2011 and 2015, we kept ourselves busy music-wise, mostly by playing on each other's various solo projects. Gigs were sporadic; there were tours to promote James' heavy soul album *Love Undercover* and Ian's psychedelic opus *Cut From A Star*.

A line-up change: Lee Southall stays in Hebden Bridge to continue with a solo album he'd been nurturing since the start of the break. We draft in Paul Molloy who we've known for a long time and had been playing with Ian in the Serpent Power band.

Ian and Molloy also formed a swamp rock'n'roll outfit that took them up and down the furthest and most forgotten regions of Britain. Duffy played bass for a few bands, and the foundations of the Skeleton Key label were laid.

We'd rotate with DJ sessions and acoustic sets at a local bar, The Coda Maine, which was one of those brilliant, lawless venues that you suddenly come to your senses in in the breaking light, feeling as if you've spent the past 12 hours on the furthest reaches of some outer dimension.

I wrote a couple of books, moved in with my girlfriend, Aja, and recorded with The Lost Brothers and Bill Ryder-Jones on the *New Songs Of Dawn And Dust* album. Most of the time I wandered around thinking up ways to keep up with the rent.

After being in the band since we were kids, the break in Coral activity soon had us restless. We'd all left school and gone straight into the band, we weren't qualified to do much else. The only way I can describe it is that the world outside looked like Castle Grayskull.

When the decision was made to start bouncing ideas around for a new album, we moved fast. We wrote six songs in as many weeks and had them studio-ready in half the time.

We could see the road ahead again, it was clear and flat, as if emerging from a wilderness.

CAVES

With a tour on the horizon, it's agreed we'll have to get the rehearsal room back into some kind of working shape. In the five-year break between albums, we'd ended up sharing it with bands we know from around our area. The Sundowners, By The Sea, She Drew The Gun. In that time, it had fallen into disrepair; sockets hanging out of the plasterboard, broken lights, a toilet that wouldn't flush. We decide to re-establish contact with Tonto; bring him up from Devon for a week. He'd only need that to do a month's worth of work.

Tonto had been our touring guitar tech for the period 2006-'11. We covered some distance together, mainly across Europe and the UK. You might have seen him at a gig from that period, watching over the stage like a Comanche chief.

Two years into his tenure with us, we'd decided to move all our equipment from Liverpool back to our hometown. Steve 'Adge' Atherton had found us a room beyond a set of railway lines on an industrial estate and we were quick to snap it up.

Tonto virtually hand-built the room himself. He converted it from a draughty corrugated space above a car garage into a soundproofed studio, complete with carpets and multicoloured spaceship-like spotlight panels that hung from ceiling beams like giant manta-rays.

He was meticulous too, especially in his use of Velcro. It was everywhere. On the floors, the walls. Underneath amplifiers. If you took your shoes off, you'd get stuck somewhere. It was super strength, Ecto-Velcro. Everything had its place and he wanted it to stay there.

In the early days of the band, we'd rehearsed in the top bedroom of the house James and Ian lived in. There were murals covering the walls, cut-outs from music magazines that they'd stuck up with Blu-Tac. The Who, Oasis, Otis Redding, The Ronettes. You'd be surrounded by them.

Things changed when we moved over to the city, a dark windowless warehouse on Dale Street called Crash Studios. It was a new lease of life at first because you had the run of the place; you could rehearse at whatever volume you liked, drink at the small downstairs bar, play pool and smoke in the rooms. But those rooms were tough to spend longer than four hours in, and when the opportunity came to move home, we jumped at it.

The new room in Hoylake is on a place they call 'the forgotten estate' because the railway barriers fall every 15 minutes or so, which can leave fire and ambulance crews at the mercy of the trains.

After moving our gear there, we began decorating it with film and music posters: *The Wicker Man*, *Blade Runner*. A huge figurine from *Alien* still in its box. Lounge music album sleeves. Billie Holiday, Link Wray, The Stooges. Robbie Fowler. The Banana Splits. A huge painting of Toshiro Mifune in *Seven Samurai*.

A partitioned room at the back has a Tascam eight-track tape machine rigged into an amplifier, the equipment that *The Curse Of Love* album was recorded on. Another smaller room has shelves full of *Judge Dredd* and *Hellblazer* comics, cheap rock'n'roll CD compilations where the backing tracks have been overdubbed with 80s synths. A Sega Master System and stacks of old games.

Anyway, Tonto comes up and sleeps on the couch. He cleans the rehearsal room from top to bottom, rewires all the electrics and fixes a couple of faulty amplifiers. I realise after he's gone that the toilet actually flushes again and the light is back on in the fridge. He works two days straight and refuses to take any money. And with that, at the stroke of midnight, he packs up his tools and sets off for the six-hour drive back to Devon.

I hadn't been there when he left. There was a message on my phone from James to say they'd finished with the clean-up and to come and see if everything was ok with the keyboards.

I trudge over the railway lines in the dark, across the muddy dirt track and the floodlit football fields; the clubhouse and faded boards that advertise Thwaites, Bushmills, Hoylake Transit. I walk past the panel-beater's yard and the truck depot. You can hear the wind shuddering through the units at night. I'm always glad to get to the small front door of our building.

I run up the stairs and walk in. The place is transformed. Everything is back in its correct place, as it was when we'd first moved there, and the room is plush with the smell of fresh Velcro.

Hoylake, 04/01/16

REHEARSAL DAY 3

I walk to the room with Duffy. He tells me about a soundtrack he's been working on for an animation. A short, surreal film that contains no dialogue. He says he's been recording it in his front room and it was a pain because the microphone picks up everything from the terraced street that we both live on.

James and Ian are already there when we arrive, stooped over an Ace Tone drum machine, manipulating the speed of the rhythm, an exotic mambo that you imagine might underpin some kind of Hawaiian death ballad, possibly.

There is an old Lowry keyboard stacked in the corner. A huge thing that sits on a single speaker. Bright coloured buttons and circular dials jump out from every angle. The type of thing you'd see in black and white footage of Blackpool dancehalls. I move toward it, pull up a stool and flick a couple of switches. I'm never really sure what sound it will make. Today it sounds like the harpsichord from that vampire flick *Suspiria*.

Behind me, the thud of bass brings to life, and at this point I know that the car mechanics directly below us will know that we're here. They might bounce up the staircase at some point and tell us to keep the volume down.

Molloy shows up and plugs in, uses a slide that gives a similar sound to something from the *Plastic Ono Band* album. And we'll not be sure what song we're playing or what the chords are until we hear the lead vocal. But we'll keep playing. Something coalesces about then. Fizzes up from the floor until you can sense it in your backbone, your fingers. It comes together.

And we can all feel it, a shared sense that it's good to be working together as a unit. This is how songs are born.

Hoylake, 14/01/16

CASSETTE COMPS

They are compiled devoutly through long afternoons. Cold nights in the winter. Stacks of vinyl and dust sleeves scattered about the room. We draw front covers in black biro and pass them between each other. Give them names: *Zoosty 3000. Space Exotica. Border Town Ghost. Tropical Midnight. Gwigway. The Rhythm Kid.* We obsess over track listings. 3am in the kitchen with headphones on. Everywhere asleep.

Through long car journeys, we listen through warped tape decks; the warmth of magnetism in the bass end, the haunted hiss in the high. We listen and listen again, and slowly ideas appear. Tapes, CDs, online playlists. They all go in. Shoeboxes full of TDK and Maxell in the attic. Sometimes they disappear, only to return years later in the rehearsal room under a pile of *Big Trouble In Little China* figurines.

The cassette comp is where, essentially, the first seed of any Coral album is sewn.

PARIS PRESS WEEKEND

"Five bells pick up," the text said last night. "BE READY."

It's dawn and I'm rifling through a kitchen drawer for my passport. I hear the diesel chug of a Hackney outside, then the cabbie raps on the door and I leap at the latch to open it, so not to wake the whole street.

There isn't much chat on the way to the airport. *Hotline Bling* is straining through the radio so I pull my hat over my ears and try and get some sleep before the flight.

James and I get to Manchester early, and arrive in Paris before noon. The runway outside is icy. A man holding a placard greets us and ushers us into a cab.

Ray meets us at the hotel. Ray is the delegate from the record label. He's tall, dressed all in black with a greased rug of black hair that ends above his collar. He alternates between tokes on an E-cigarette and a roll-up. Ray is from Dublin and tells us he'll miss our concert in April because he's going to Cheltenham to "lose a fuck-load of money." He speaks broken French to the female barmaids, and any time I ask him for a beer throughout the day, he laughs through the gap in his front teeth, and says, "*Splendid.*"

Our purpose for being here is to promote the new album. Interviews, radio sessions. Most of the interviews happen in a back room of the hotel, a bare room with two dark green Chesterfield couches and a couple of tables. The rest of the hotel is like some soft porn film set; red painted walls and locked 'private' rooms. Framed LUI magazine covers on the wall. Brigitte Bardot. Jane Birkin. Kate Moss. Lara Stone. It's hard to get anywhere in the hotel because you're bombarded with these images and find yourself rooted to the spot in a corridor, staring at the wall like some sedated inpatient.

We're waiting it out in the Chesterfield room now, until the first interviewer arrives. It's two in the afternoon here, and we're not long off the plane. Two journalists appear at the door with rucksacks and recording equipment and we beckon them in.

French journalists tend to stand out from most others. You remember a French interview because you've been forced to divert from whatever spiel you've prepared, which is no bad thing by any means; they're mostly well prepared and knowledgeable. But it can wind up more like a psychotherapy session than an interview.

Sophie and Felix from *Rolling Stone* want to know about dream colours. Annette mentions the experimental music of Erik Satie. Philippe talks about inspiration and enlightenment and Vivienne from *Les InRock* wants us to play Marcel Proust's word association game.

The interviews come thick and fast. When one is about to end, another journalist appears meekly at the doorway. Ray ferries them over by their shoulders and sits them down. They fumble through bags for recording equipment and scribbled notes.

After dinner, the whole thing starts again. We repeat ourselves after a while, as we've been talking solidly since about noon. Around midnight, we end up with Ray and some of the French record label in the smoking area of a Paris bar with those overhead halogen heaters. Everything is hot and cold at the same time and when I look at my watch it's 1am.

I wake up with my clothes on. It's still dark outside and I'd only come to my room to get tobacco, I think, before nodding off. I'm thirsty, so run my mouth under the tap in the bathroom, but then decide I'm still after a proper drink. I exit the room and back into the tiny Art Deco pulley-lift and glide down to the ground floor.

I move toward the bar and find it empty, except for Ray, who's hunched over his laptop in the deserted seating area that leads to the foyer.

He sees me and looks up, and asks if he can help. I tell him I'm only looking for a shot or a beer, and Ray nods to the bar, smiles that half smile and says, "*Splendid*."

Back in the single room, a couple next door are making the headboard shake and I'm squinting at the ceiling trying to stop it from spinning, thinking this is only supposed to happen in films.

Paris, 18/01/16

CIRCUITRY

Tonight in rehearsal, we resurrect *She Sings The Mourning* for the tour. Midway through playing the song there's a weird electrical surge which makes the overhead lights dim for a second or two, flicker, then spring back to life suddenly. This happens five or six times. The light fittings are swinging too, as if someone has opened a window or door. We play right through it. It's as if the flickering of the lights coincides perfectly with the motorik rhythm of the song.

We lifted that tune from Krautrock bands such as Can and Neu!, and I always feel there's some kind of supernature at work when we play it.

On this occasion, the song takes on a new eeriness. It becomes some kind of hypnosis ritual that has us locked in. Séance-like.

It defies explanation, the power surge. We'd had everything rewired a few days earlier when Tonto serviced the room. It was all in good shape.

When an electrician looks it over the following day, he's stumped: "I've seen this type of thing around here before in these units," he says, "but I can't get to the bottom of it. It's like there are *ghosts in the circuitry.*"

Hoylake, 22/01/16

ADVENTURELAND

A national music magazine want to photograph us while we're dressed as fishermen. If we don't want to do that, we can stand in front of the Liver Buildings and look out to the Mersey. They think it'll look good, they say, for people who are unfamiliar with the band and want a taste of what we're about. We're not so keen on the idea, and spend half an hour going through alternate locations.

After a short interview in Parr Street Studio, we suggest going over to New Brighton for the shoot, nearer where we live. There's a promenade there with amusements and arcades. Victorian parks with bandstands and blue plaques celebrating early Beatles concerts. A small museum dedicated to the Merseybeat star Rory Storm.

You can see Liverpool clearly from the promenade, the old docks mainly, at Bootle and Seaforth, the brand new gargantuan container cranes that have been shipped over from Korea. They dominate the skyline like giant red painted skeletons, dwarf the Chinese and Dutch shipping freighters that amble drowsily into port.

On arrival, the photographer is inspired. We find a bandstand in Vale Park, which is painted brilliant white, with huge pillars that prop up a dome roof. We start the shoot there. After a time, we're happy with the pictures and decide to move on.

The wind gets up. We move toward Fort Perch, a pre-war coastal defence battery, built to defend the port of Liverpool. Made with huge sandstone breezeblocks, it looks like a small castle. The grey river pounds against its north-facing wall.

On the east side, the tide is pushing in. It sprays onto a pebbled path that leads out to a tall lighthouse. We decide we'll do the last shoot here. As we're being battered by the spray from the sea, the photographer is trying to hand us an umbrella to use as a prop, but the idea is laughed away.

After the shoot, we shake hands with the photographer and the journalist, and they leave for their trains. We cross the road and duck into Legends Café Bar, which is wedged between a huge amusement arcade called Adventureland, and a chip shop that has its steel shutters pulled to the ground. As it's still winter, the promenade is fairly desolate.

We sit down and drink tea from polystyrene cups. I order a portion of chips, but "the fryer is misbehaving," the man behind the counter says.

In Adventureland, we mooch happily around the slots and arcades, pose for stupid phone photos on broken rides. There's nobody around. We have the run of the place. What's eerie is that everything is working as if it were packed with people. The arcades. The penny pushers. The teddy pickers. Everything lit up. There's something about it that reminds me of the early days of being in the band. I don't know why.

As the sky darkens on the way to the train station, we get to talking about the old nightclubs that used to inhabit the promenade. The Chelsea Reach club, which was notorious for admitting underage kids. It was almost a rite of passage to go to The Chelsea around here if you were nearing the last year of school.

It's a funny train journey home. Molloy had left us earlier to go to the nearby cinema to watch *The Revenant* with his girlfriend, Fiona. So it was just the four of us. James, Ian, Duffy, me. We go over some of the weirder gigs some of us have been a part of. In the period between albums, a couple of the band played in a group called The Viper Kings, a rock'n' roll covers band. They'd played gigs in places that their singer, Neville, had secured. Places like Skegness, Minehead, Harrogate. They'd done a few gigs in Butlin's, too. One of the gigs was for an 80s themed fancy dress night. Another was an afternoon matinee. Another time they were booked into a biker's convention. All the bikers were on speed and they had to "amp up the psycho level" on the particular brand of rock'n'roll they played. They did John Mayall's *I'm Your Witch Doctor* and that won the audience over.

It would make a good film, I offer, and then someone says that if it ever got made, it should be called *The Arsehole Of The North*.

I decide there and then that I'll write this movie, and it will cover The Viper Kings' apocalyptic tour of Minehead Butlin's, Skegness and Harrogate, and I'll document it exactly the way it happened.

New Brighton, 27/01/16

DASH

A journalist from *The Guardian* came to interview us today. He was from Leeds way, he said, near Otley, and said that the drive down the motorway had been terrible because of a nasty blizzard. The newspaper wanted to do a piece on us using the rehearsal room as a backdrop. Take some photographs and get a feel for our world.

I find it weird usually, when journalists come to the room. They tend to wander around staring at the walls. The huge *Murders In The Rue Morgue* poster as you walk in. They seem interested initially, but I always feel like they're itching to get away. Maybe I'm wrong.

We talked for an hour. The journalist wanted to know what influenced the new album, where the lyrics come from. James talked Richard Yates novels and the surreal photography of Gregory Crewdson, Texas psych and how hard it is to tour America at the moment. We talked about vintage equipment and how it compares to modern equipment. We talked about an exhibition we're planning which will feature the artwork Ian has dreamed up for the *Distance Inbetween* sleeve. We talked about the early line-up of The Wailers, how it was Peter, Bunny and Bob, and they achieved a sort of high magic when they sang together. How they were a gang, and music to us has mostly been about gangs. We talked music, football, British horror films and the Kardashians.

Hoylake, 29/01/15

OVERHEARD INTERVIEW PIECE

"...some of the songs even stretch to four or five minutes now, which is like prog rock for us."

"Why do you think that is?"

"I'm not sure... I think we've always had a weird condensed grasp of time. Songs in the past that we thought were psychedelic soundscapes turned out to be three minute jingles when we'd come to get the album mastered."

"That's so strange. And this spookiness, where does that derive from? It's almost like that funfair sound, you know, Del Shannon's *Runaway*. That type of thing."

"That's the slap-back. The sound of the tape. There are boatyards where we live, loads of them. You hear the wind rattling the topmasts at night. They give a certain echo, which is an impression of a real thing, essentially. The same as a shadow. I think that's where the music exists. In the afterthought, or the subconscious. The echoes, or memories."

Parr Street Studios, 03/02/16

FEATURE-LENGTH

Earth Wind And Fire founder member Maurice White has today passed away. - The Daily Mirror

Midweek afternoon in the rehearsal room. We're throwing around ideas for music videos. There will be at least three singles from the new album, each needing its own set of visuals. Recently, we've been working with a great director, Dominic Foster, who conjures these halogen bright VHS mini-movies that look as if they've been beamed in from some pirate TV station on Neptune.

The idea for *Chasing The Tail Of A Dream* springs from computer animator John Whitney and his experimental films from the 70s. We decide Miss Fortune would suit something more British. The early years of psychedelia, Pink Floyd's *See Emily Play*, or *Penny Lane.*

The band themselves had been directing their own B-movies long before I joined. They'd been making them since they were kids. Some are takes on existing Hollywood films. Others are more stream-of-consciousness experiments.

The feature-length films include:

Mannequin (Horror)

Lazy Rider (*Easy Rider* on BMXs)

Bobby Zeus and the Youngbloods (*Behind The Music* doc.)

The Loneliest Pier (Art house)

Nightfreak (Music)

Shadow Weaver (Kung-Fu/ cross dresser)

Goofo (Kitchen sink drama)

Scarecrow (Horror)

Hoylake, 05/02/16

CLICK-CLACK

The record label has asked us each to put a playlist together. To post online for fans, they say. A glimpse of what we're listening to. I'm on the train between Conway Park and Hamilton Square when I get the message, so I think up a theme based around railroad songs:

Chuck Berry – *Downbound Train*
Alan Vega – *Jukebox Babe*
Vashti Bunyan – *Train Song*
Captain Beefheart – *Click Clack*
The Kinks – *Last Of The Steam-Powered Trains*
John Hammond – *2:19*
The Beach Boys – *Cabinessence*
Kevin Morby – *Slow Train*
The Smiths – *Nowhere Fast*
Bo Diddley – *Down Home Special*
13th Floor Elevators – *Roller Coaster* (live, 1966)
Kraftwerk – *Trans-Europe Express*

Birkenhead, 12/02/16

HAIRY PANIC

There is a strange, ghostly new type of tumbleweed sweeping across Australia. It's blocking people into their homes. They've called it 'Hairy Panic'. - The Daily Telegraph

Management send over early reviews of the album, which are good across the board. You try not to pander to the press too much, but it's undeniable that positive reviews are good for an album, and the knock-on effect.

Later, on the 5pm train to Liverpool, I'm reading *The Real Cool Killers* by Chester Himes. He's like Raymond Chandler, but instead of LA, his stories are set in black Harlem. His characters have names like Coffin Ed and Gravedigger Jones. It's really great stuff, detective noir, but not in the obvious way.

I meet up with James and Ian, who've been recording a session in Parr Street studio. We eat burritos and they tell me about a live album they have planned, featuring all of the artists on the Skeleton Key label. We get midweek-drunk and it's a struggle to leave for the last train.

It's cold when I alight for the walk home. The lighthouse has a white painted scar down its belly, like a stalactite. The gritter is out on the main road. I see its laboured gait and yellow light approaching. It volleys a hail of shingle and gravel at my shins as it passes, and it stings momentarily. Tomorrow, back to the rehearsal room to give the set a run-through before the tour starts, two weeks to the day.

Hoylake, 19/02/16

CRIME MOVIE THEMES

Conrad from management gets in touch to ask if I'll put together a playlist for Napster to share on their website. I draw up some crime movie themes and send them over.

Roy Budd – *Get Carter*
John Barry – *The Ipcress File*
The Handsome Family – *Far From Any Road* (*True Detective*)
Lalo Schifrin – *Bullit*
Curtis Mayfield – *Pusherman*
Roy Budd – *Free Tarrant* (*The Black Windmill*)
Mikis Theodorakis – *Theme From Serpico*
James Brown – *The Boss*
David Shire – *The Taking Of Pelham One Two Three*
Tony Bennett – *Rags To Riches* (*Goodfellas*)

27/02/16

THE GREAT VOID

We've reached that in-between point while we're waiting for the tour to start. At this stage you tend to mope around, wondering what to do. You might iron some underwear or make a playlist for a long motorway journey. Watch the clock tick. Wait it out in a pub.

I listen to a band comp called *The Road I'm On,* which was being passed around at the time of the *Butterfly House* album. It features 70s troubadours like Tim Hardin and Townes Van Zandt, Annie Briggs and Karen Dalton.

In bed I drift off to sleep thinking about the time just before we were signed.

The Skellys ran a pub in the centre of Liverpool around then, which most of us ended up working in so we could pay the rehearsal room rent. We used to obsess over music while emptying the bins at the end of a Saturday night or taking the deliveries in the morning.

You'd go from there, back to whoever's house and sit up smoking weed, listening back to cassette recordings of us rehearsing.

I remember us watching *Pink Floyd: Live At Pompeii* one time and feeling like my mind had been split open for weeks after.

The same week, we heard Beefheart's *Safe As Milk* in Duffy's top bedroom and James wrote the brunt of *Skeleton Key*. *Shadows Fall* came not long after, then *I Remember When* showed up after we hallucinated that the sea had frozen.

We'd go seamlessly into Phil Spector-inspired songs that sounded like the *Mean Streets* soundtrack, the tin-pan alley girl groups, who we loved. Everything we did was connected by the desire to escape. Escape jobs, escape reality.

I recognised that feeling as I nodded off. Almost like it had returned. That connection, the means to escape again. It was through music, and always would be.

Hoylake, 28/02/16

IN SESSION, BBC RADIO 6 MUSIC

We're on the 9 o'clock train from Lime Street to Euston, headed toward Maida Vale for a BBC6 session with Steve Lamacq. We're dotted about the carriage on different seats, settling into the journey.

I've been offered to DJ at some after show parties on the upcoming tour. A couple of promoters in Glasgow and Sheffield are interested. I mostly have to play for about an hour and then hang around for a bit. On tour, you have to make a clean break for it sometimes, before it gets into the early hours. Keep your stamina up. Remind yourself you're there to earn a bit of extra money. It's weird, most people automatically think you're flush because you've "been on the telly." On arrival in Euston, we're ferried by taxi between radio stations where we talk DJs through the album, track-by-track. The consensus is that this is a comeback, and we're happy to go with it, as it's a good starting point for an interview. We finish up and jump in a car toward the studio for tonight's session.

The BBC building in Maida Vale is a strange place. It's a vast, windowless network of secret doors, unmarked corridors and underground studios. The place is a labyrinth. Steve Lamacq arrives eventually, and we shake hands. He comes off as a little tougher than you'd imagine. James says, "If he likes a band, he'll back them unequivocally and I admire that, especially as a modern radio DJ. There aren't many of his kind left."

There is a short interview where we talk about Hawkwind and British psychedelia. The new album gets a once-over, and before we know it, he's introducing the set.

We play for high stakes. From the first note, we're supercharged. Not fast as such, but heavy. I think it's a release of tension. It goes down pretty well. There is a crowd of competition winners who stare down from a mezzanine, who respond well to the new songs. They're ushered out as soon as we finish, before we make a dash to the train station.

On the train, talk turns to He-Man figures, Bill Gates' parents, the worst Beatles album *(With The Beatles)* and something called a *Trumpalumpa*, which is a made-up hybrid between Donald Trump and an oompa-loompa. Within five minutes, we've phoned an artist who photoshops the image and sends it back. It's posted online. I can't stop laughing at it.

I wake up to the sound of the train manager announcing our arrival into Lime Street. As we alight, I bump into Dave Kay, our original live sound engineer. We share a cab with him. As we dip into the Kingsway tunnel, we're half-drunkenly reminiscing about the first tour of America, being snowed in in Colorado and the day off on the Canadian border. Dave says, "Remember that day at Niagara Falls when one of you made a pair of flip-flops out of a cardboard box and gaffer tape, to prevent your new shoes from getting soaked? And the waterproof ponchos and the beer and The Maid Of The Mist ferrying us out to the hidden Horseshoe Falls… I've got the photos in the house somewhere, stuffed between boxes in the new attic… I'm certain they exist."

Liverpool, 02/03/16

TOUR PRE-PRODUCTION

Sam whistles up the stairs with a projector under his arm, greeting everybody with his free hand. I ask him, "Weren't you at Liverpool Psych Festival last year?" And he tells me yeah, he did most of the visuals that day, and then instantly I know we're onto a good thing. Sam's been drafted in to do lights on the tour

Within minutes, he's hoisted the box projector on top of a piece of tall scaffold and is beaming a spotlight onto a huge white crinkled sheet that hangs behind the stage.

We're having a final rehearsal in the Academy building next door to Lime Street station. The first date of the tour is tomorrow, in Newcastle, and there are creases in the set that need ironing out.

Most of us are still tired from last night's journey back from the capital. The running argument is whether the theme from 80s TV show *Pugwall* has the same guitar sound as *Anarchy In The UK*. It passes the time.

Sam's lights are exceptional. He's synced his *Lawnmower Man*-meets-*Tron* visual style with our whole set. Each visual has its own mood, its own movement that corresponds with whatever song we're playing. The instrumental section at the end of *Million Eyes* looks like

Kubrick's *2001* Stargate scene. It changes to *Tetsuo: Iron Man* for *Fear Machine*. I'm meant to be playing the keyboards, but my eyes are hopelessly drawn to the colourama.

The stage itself looks great. We're using these great vintage-looking mustard amplifiers. All the amps on stage are small, and it looks like some old Nashville set up. With the analogue synths at the side of the stage, we look like a kind of sci-fi Buddy Holly covers band.

After we play, I leave the venue and do some last-minute shopping before catching a packed train home. At home I keep listening to the radio in the hope of hearing our new single. I'll sit there for an hour in the morning, willing it to come on. When it finally gets played, I pick the whole thing apart. And then when it finishes, I jump up and turn the radio off and carry on with the day.

Hoylake, 03/03/16

CHAPTER TWO

UK TOUR

UK tour begins. The Angel Of The North. Dolph Lundgren movies. In-store signings. The lone wolf. A bear-man in Birmingham. Manta Rays in Notts. Viola Beach tribute. Ian Brown in a servo.

ANGEL OF THE NORTH

'11.15 PICK UP AT THE SHIP INN.' The text comes early, around 8am though I'm awake before then. It's the first day of the tour and I'm determined to do it properly this time. Eat well. Keep hangovers at bay. We've done too many tours of not eating or sleeping to know by the end of it you want to pack the whole thing in. It affects the way you play, too.

Big John is on tour manager duties. We know him from way back when he used to drive The Hokum Clones around. He's a great driver, and stands six foot four in his Adidas.

John is flanked on the passenger side by Carl. Carl is on merch duties, and is a well known face around town in the record and comic shops. He worked at Hairy Records for a while, and when we first moved to Liverpool we'd frequent that dusty cellar packed with second-hand vinyl, tapes and CDs. I once swapped a copy of *Fools Gold* on gold-coloured vinyl in there for a Mills Brothers record and a Lee Perry twelve-inch. I got a good deal on that. Carl's a music and comic encyclopedia.

The motorways are laced with snow this morning. It's brisk and wintery and we turn the heating up in the van, as we can see our breath as we talk.

Somebody asks when should we start the 'Lungathon', which is basically a marathon of Dolph Lundgren movies played back to back. In the end, *The Larry Sanders Show* wins and we watch from episode one. Conversation veers seamlessly into the question of who would win in a fight between Mick Hucknall and Marti Pellow. After an argument, it's agreed Pellow would come out on top, being a Glaswegian and all. Hucknall would melt. And so the hours roll away. Eventually, we drift into Newcastle, beautiful city of bridges. We come in slow, through Gateshead and my eyes are drawn to the names of pubs and shops, as they always are in unfamiliar towns: S n' S Hair. Envisage. Tattoo Mania. Gateshead Snooker Centre. Somebody points toward the horizon and says, "There's the high level bridge in *Get Carte*r that Michael Caine vaults off to escape."

Things start well. The place is rammed, and The Cut Glass Kings do a good job of warming the punters up with their own take on Birmingham Sabbath-fuzz via Ray Davies. Neon Waltz are next, all the way from Wick at the top of Scotland, and their strange outsider carousel tunes chime well with the listening audience. We go on to respectful applause and throughout the show the crowd don't really move out of that catatonic state. Still, Newcastle's a tough one for any 'guitar' band, and the post-show reports are good.

Before the journey that day, I'd asked Big John to let me know when we were passing The Angel Of The North on the motorway. I'd nodded off at some point, before somebody nudged me and said, "There you go, Nick," and I jumped up and wiped the condensation from the window just in time to see the back of her wings throw a shadow across the surrounding green, the beautiful iron siren sucking in awe and wonder and magic and reflecting it back down to the south where some assume this is a land of perpetual darkness.

Newcastle, 04/03/16

DVDs FOR TOURBUS

The Lost Boys

Dig!

Command Performance

The Larry Sanders Show (series one)

Ghoulies Go To College

The Fog

Jason And The Argonauts

Doug Stanhope: No Refunds

Cream Farewell Concert

American Folk Blues Festival

Pentathlon

The American Friend

GLASGOW

I wake in a motorway Travelodge in one of those tiny camp beds that go hammock-shaped after a couple of hours. Big John took the king-sized because of this morning's drive to Glasgow. I'm watching *The Hound Of The Baskervilles* on the small wall-mounted TV. I'm glad to waste away an hour or so like this while I wake up.

Dave from management phones to say the new album is at Number 4 in the midweek chart and they expect it to drop to around seven, which seems pretty good. I'd almost forgotten the Top Forty even existed any more.

John leaves to drive the van around from the car park. I shower and dress and run out in search of food. I bump into the rest of the band in reception. There's not much around here, so we cross a motorway bridge and I grab a vegetable pasty from Greggs, you know, to stay on the healthy side.

Back on the motorway, we pass the Angel again and I see her face this time. The smooth ridges like the gills of a fish. Rooted to the spot like that, like an old pagan god.

Around lunchtime, somewhere past the border, it's decided that if all of our DNA were to be combined, the resulting hybrid would look exactly like Noel Edmonds. His features apparently take in elements from all of our faces.

On the van stereo, we listen to Muddy Waters' *After The Rain* and then ZZ Top's 1973 album *Très Hombres*. Tex-mex via the Hells Angels. We're bursting up the motorway with it ripping through the speakers. Before long we're seeing signs for EASTERHOUSE, and passing huge skeletal gas rings and tower blocks that clump together like four pronged concrete plugs pushing against the sky; Glasgow's sobering russet-red sky that sends out a warning: *Be ready*.

The gig itself is one of the best we've ever done. Crowds don't come much better than a Saturday night in Glasgow. There are people being passed, *flung* over people's heads. It feels like a real comeback here.

I'm DJ'ing tonight in the west end, a place called The Record Factory. After a short taxi ride, I chat with the promoter in the back room and we square up on the fee.

I play one song – Bowie's *Sound And Vision,* before giving up. Molloy and Duffy arrive. The Cut Glass Kings and Neon Waltz are here, and our mate Keggo. He's swigging a four-pint carton of milk from the rider as he walks through the crowd. They think it's hilarious that I've only played one tune, but I explain that I've been promoting the gig for a month so it's more about getting heads through the door. The in-house DJ takes over.

The next few hours are a blur. We're stood by the bar mostly, and the drinks are free, and the place is rammed. There are two ambulances outside, and three people are helped into them, though I'm not sure what for. Friends turn up. Neon Waltz. Lee and the lads from a band called Rituals. A masseuse called Annabelle who is offering free acupuncture. We stay until the early hours, only deciding to shoot off when the first hint of daylight appears.

The hotel is forty-five minutes away, above a pub in a place called Wishaw, where John Higgins, the snooker player is from. When we arrive, there are two police cars pulled up and people spilling out of the pub. We mill through the crowd to our rooms and I spend the night shivering, wide-awake in a tiny bed, slugging watery beer to try and knock myself out.

Glasgow 05/03/16

WORKINGMEN'S

Monday in the van. It's subdued after the Glasgow session and we pass time talking about plans for a new album. It feels like we're on a roll at the moment and it would be good to start kicking some ideas around for new songs. Duffy is in the front seat, flicking through a comp he's made up of soundtrack music: Goblin, The Soundcarriers, Ennio Morricone, the theme from *Twin Peaks*.

We're playing a small venue in Leeds called the Brudenell Social Club tonight, which is an old workingmen's club in the middle of a housing estate. It's a legendary and brilliant venue, but it's slightly too small to fit our full light show in.

I played here with The Sundowners a couple of years ago. Before the gig we were parked up at the back, watching an old man giving haircuts to his friends. They were queuing up to sit on this old stool he'd wedged into the ground at the back of the club. And then he'd draw a pair of clippers round the back and sides of their heads, and leave them looking like they'd just escaped a house fire.

On the way up, we'd toyed with watching a film called *Ninja The Protector,* but decided, "It looks too shit, even by our standards." Instead, we had music all the way up: *My White Bicycle*, *Arnold Layne* and The Black Angels' *Bad Vibrations* were the memorable cuts. I'm in the mood to perform by the time we arrive and the place is filling up already.

After soundcheck, Glyn, the promotions rep, offers to drop us into town for food. We get out at a restaurant we were banking on being open, but find that it's closed down. It has that white sponge paint covering the windows. We decide to venture further into town, and eventually find an old Italian place.

After a good meal, we wait for a lift back to the social club in the underpass where we were dropped off. There's an old man with white hair in the same doorway where we wait. He's wearing brown brogues, a blue suit and a white rain mac. He's holding a bunch of flowers. There is a gang of kids sitting at a nearby bus stop, dressed in black hiking coats and caps.

A blonde woman in a miniskirt approaches, and she kisses the old man on the cheek. She's a good few years younger than him, maybe forty, and talks in a Russian accent. He hands her the flowers and she accepts them awkwardly. The kids twig it as the couple walk across the road. They think the woman is an escort. They seem to be happy for the old guy, even call out to him as they walk. "Fill your boots," one of them shouts, and he turns, gives a look of recognition and raises his hand. The kids laugh.

My brother Liam's band, By The Sea, play tonight. They do well in Leeds and there are a good few people there to see them. They sound like the *Drive* movie soundtrack, or The Pale Fountains by way of an 80s arcade game. Marvin Powell goes on before them. He's a Jackson C Frank-style singer on the Skeleton Key label, and plays a great set with his new band.

I'm beginning to think this tour is becoming a tale of two crowds. On one hand, they go ballistic and on the other, take on a kind of hypnotised expression, glued to the projections. Tonight they seem quite subdued.

One thing I've learned about playing to a static audience is you've got to come out swinging, or you'll back yourself into a dead-end.

It looks like we're about to turn it around when the lead guitar amp blows. After that, the show is racked with sound problems. We have to leave the stage forty minutes or so into the gig because of the faulty amp. The guitar techs are in the dim light of the stage corridor, torches and screwdrivers in hand, searching for the source of the problem. The crowd are getting restless outside and all anyone is saying is, "If Tonto was here, if Tonto was here..."

Leeds, 07/03/16

MAP OF VEINS

Sometimes it'll start with a title. A painting or a film, maybe. *Arabian Sand. A Warning To The Curious*. It might be something overheard in a nearby conversation. *Pass It On*. Or a misheard lyric. *All The Birds Have Flown*. Lines from books. "*Like Miranda said, life's not for the dead*". Sometimes it'll be the simplest of feelings said directly. That type of song tends to speak for itself.

If I get an idea for some words I might send them to James, who'll pair it with some chord shape, some riff lifted from Roky Erickson and flipped on its head, possibly. The idea will germinate slowly, and we'll email it back and forth, building the thing into a working shape.

Other times he'll show up at rehearsal with a song all the way finished and it'll be about complementing what's already there, letting it breathe.

White Bird was written mostly by Ian in his top floor flat. Ian and James worked it through and the three of us finished it in my house one night after they'd brought it to rehearsal.

Duffy will usually take a rough recording of a song home and work out an arrangement for harmonies on his own.

This is how the brunt of *Distance Inbetween* was written.

NOTTINGHAM BOUND/ THREE WAY CONVERSATION

"That's an unbelievable Mick Jagger impression."

"I can't breathe. That's so funny, like. "

"You've got to start high up in your nose, up here, that's what people forget. Then you move deeper... *everyone cool it yeah.*"

"Ah, that's hurting my ribs that."

"I need to get that Rolling Stones live DVD back."

"Which one?"

"The one you lent to Noel Gallagher. From about '84. When Jagger sings *Paint It Black* about nine octaves too low."

"Was that when he'd just finished filming *Freejack*?"

"Yeah, what a movie."

"And the stage set-up was like a future dystopia, exactly like *Freejack*."

"Yeah, but with a massive inflatable dick on the stage that doesn't tie in with any of the industrial stuff."

"Oh my god. Yes."

"His 80s and 90s periods are his best. He's a fucking lunatic by then. Lunatic."

"That *Being Mick* documentary."

"Well funny. *Why don't you get a gun and shoot it through this heart of mine...*"

"Is that where Lenny Kravitz makes him a cheese toastie?"

"Yeah, it's got the making of the *God Gave Me Everything* video as well."

"Hahahahaha."

"It's a belter tune. Cracks me up. I can watch him all day. There are some stinkers on that album though. Some absolute fucking stinkers."

Motorway, 08/03/16

MANTA-RAY

A couple of us have a chance meeting with Ian Brown at a motorway service station after Big John pulls in for breakfast. Ian says he's staying nearby, and The Stone Roses are rehearsing and recording their new single not far from here. It's news to me; I wasn't even aware they were doing one. What's better is he confirms we'll be supporting them at a concert in The Etihad Stadium, which holds around sixty thousand people. He casually slips in that we'll be sharing the bill with Public Enemy, too. So as mornings in Lymm motorway services go, it's been pretty eventful.

We get moving and talk about bringing in another tech due to the problems in last night's concert.

We finally get around to watching Dolph Lundgren's *Command Performance*. The film is set in Russia. Dolph's character plays a drummer in a rock band, that are performing at a concert in the Kremlin. The concert is interrupted when a rebel group storm the building and take the president's daughter hostage. Dolph is in the toilet smoking a joint when all this happens. He thinks he's hallucinating when he's first attacked, and ends up stabbing one of the rebels with a drumstick.

There's no background to Lundgren's character, who goes by the name of Joe, except for a brief, murky flashback that's never explained (or followed up). Is he ex-army? It's unclear. He seems well trained in semiautomatic weapons for a musician. The peak moment comes when Dolph sneaks back out into the auditorium. He creeps up to the PA system and cranks the volume up to maximum. Then he straps a guitar around his neck and, in slow motion, hits *the loudest chord ever heard*, which kills most of the rebels inside the building. He's completely unaffected.

Nottingham turns out to be a great city to visit. There are vintage stores, arcade rooms and secondhand record shops. We pile into a clothes emporium and try on *Uncle Buck*-style coats and daft hats. I buy a Wailers-style army shirt. We wander around for hours, eventually diving in to a tiny cafe where we eat great big bowls of pasta and lamb kofta. It's never usually this easy.

After soundcheck, we're whizzed to the Rough Trade record shop to do an in-store signing. I hear the faint echoes of *Distance Inbetween* as I approach. Seems strange to hear it being played in public after three months cooped up with it inside a studio.

We sit at tables in the back of the store and sign posters and album sleeves. Some people want a group photograph with us. It's not such a chore.

After the signing, the store manager tells us we can get up to fifty percent discount on CDs and records, and so we disperse into the aisles. The haul includes:

Hawkwind — *Space Ritual*
The Cramps — *Bad Songs For Bad People*
Echo And The Bunnymen —*Ocean Rain*

Silver Apples — *Silver Apples*
The Cramps — *Smell Of Female*
Unloved — *Guilty of Love*
Dan The Automator — *A Much Better Tomorrow*

Midway through the gig that night we create a sixth entity. It forms beneath the stage as we play, and expands out from the floor. It takes shape on the back wall like some strange fluid manta ray that breathes and writhes in rhythm with the sonics. It's a beautiful sight, only we're the only ones able to see it as the audience are static, mouths gawping toward the stage, hypnotised by the moving lights.

Nottingham, 08/03/16

INTERMISSION

- Take two baths.
- Read 16 pages of *Johnny Got His Gun.*
- Pick up cord jacket from tailor around the corner.
- Watch episode three of *The People Versus OJ Simpson.*
- Arrange CDs for Sheffield aftershow on Friday.
- Wash underwear.
- Watch news reports on the death of George Martin.
- Pretend to myself that I don't care about the album slipping from four to Number 11 in the charts.

I listen to an album I bought in Nottingham. I play it at least three times over. It's called *Guilty Of Love* by Unloved. I picked it up in the Rough Trade store after the signing we'd done in there. Apparently the guy who did the soundtrack for *True Detective* is involved. It sounds like Shadow Morton via Wu-Tang via Billie Holiday. It makes me feel good.

Hoylake 09/03/16

CATCHER

In Birmingham, I walk to the stage, late for soundcheck. The band have been there for near twenty minutes and are warming up. Ian and Duffy are locked into a kind of seamless rhythm that you can only conjure if you've played together in pub basements and garages through your teenage years.

I make my apologies and jump on stage, move towards the keyboards and plug in. The band continue playing.

Over the drums and bass, James is playing a riff that sounds like some kind of northern soul trumpet line, if The Seeds or Jimi Hendrix had got hold of it. He sings short falsetto couplets over the rolling track and makes it sound easy.

Directly opposite me, Molloy is playing on the outer realms; sci-fi reverberations that sound like something from *The Day The Earth Stood Still.*

Afterward in the dressing room I say to James, "Are you gonna do anything with that tune?"

"No," he says. "I was just messing about with it, but I'll probably jib it."

"It's good you know," I offer, "maybe fuck round with it a bit more."

"Maybe."

"Have you got a name for it?"

"Was trying something around the words *spirit catcher.*"

Birmingham, 10/03/16

FIGHT OR FLIGHT

They didn't see the bear-man at first. All they saw was movement within a sea of faces. Movement, and a plume of green-and-blue smoke that turned red under the projector light. They saw from where they were stood that the movement was somehow unnatural. The way a crowd moves with a pang of distress at its centre. They can recognise that. A blonde girl turns around and grimaces. A couple at the front edge toward the side barriers. The crowd begins to part and then a space appears. And that's when the security man in the yellow shirt jumped in.

He hadn't seen the bear-man, but the clearing had given him a direct view. *Here you are, you cunt. I've got you. Off we pop.* The security man clamped his hands to the bear-man's chest and tried to move him. The bear-man just stood there and lit the joint that was hidden between his lips, between the masses of knotted, greasy hair that grew around his head and face like weeds.

The security man tried to move him again, but he wouldn't budge. I could see him from my position on the stage. The bear-man had the LSD look, the caught-in-the-searchlights-flight-or-fight-look. The security man looked up into a face that towered over him and thought, *I have to do something.* And that's when they went for it. The security man gave it his best, way down by the bear-man's belly. And the bear-man began tossing him around like a rag-doll. It took five bouncers to eventually remove him. They almost broke a ceiling joist, as this ball of yellow mass tumbled toward the fire-exit. Then the bear-man was gone.

All this happened while I was playing the steel drum sample of *In The Morning*, a song that had been christened earlier in the day as 'unhinged pop music'. It was some sight.

That was just the beginning. The venue, the Birmingham Institute, was oversold, packed tight to the back wall. I saw small pockets of fighting break out all through the concert. It seemed everybody was on conflicting drugs. I could see some of my own family. My uncle Les was there. I could see him near the mixing desk, his white hair and huge hands cupped around a pint of Guinness, completely unaffected by the chaos. And the worst hadn't even happened yet.

It sounded like a distress call when I heard it. Like a mayday distress call blaring through the PA system. We carried on playing, slightly confused. Then the PA cut out completely. We realised it was Chris, our sound engineer. He'd been calling security over to the desk, where, as he put it, "a man out of his box on Salvia was hurling punches at the mixing console". I saw the security limp through the mass of people, fresh from their bout with the bear-man. After a tense few minutes, we resumed playing and finished the gig. Nights like this, it's decided, are what it's all about.

Birmingham, 10/03/16

JAMES' PLAYLIST/ SHEFFIELD ROUTE

Hawkwind – *Master Of The Universe*
Bruce Springsteen – *Point Blank*
Ghostface Killah – *Return Of The Savage*
Tim Hardin – *It'll Never Happen Again*
Joey Beltram – *Energy Flash*
The Drifters – *There Goes My Baby*
ZZ Top – *La Grange*
Bob Marley – *How Many Times*
The Stooges – *TV Eye*
Nat King Cole – *Nature Boy*

Snake Pass, 11/03/16

COLES CORNER

On the TV this morning, a farmer is reliving the moment he got struck by lightning in a field. He describes feeling this strange sensation like "biting into a pneumatic drill that's on fire." He still suffers from night terrors, he says, and an involuntary shaking in his left arm. He raises his left arm to the camera.

Sheffield today. The long drive across moors and valleys and fields pockmarked with snow, Snake Pass and the winding, seasick roads. The mood between us is fairly subdued, except for the odd flurry of exited chatter about last night's show.

As a band, it's agreed we really attract the *lone wolf* type of fan. It's true. You see quite a few of them stood at gigs on their own, mouthing the words. It's no bad thing, by any means. I relate to that person more than I like to admit. It's something in the music, some estrangement-thread, possibly.

The Leadmill is where we pull up. We played our first gig outside of Liverpool here, over 15 years ago. I've done some DJ spots here in the past, and have a real fondness for the venue, though, as one promoter told me on my last visit, it's "held together by glue and gaffer tape".

The dressing rooms are at the top of the dark, draughty building. We pile in and flop on old leather couches and read the old editions of *Melody Maker* that have been plastered to the wall. Everybody decides that they're bored sitting inside, and they might as well go for a wander. I decide to stay, and stretch out on the fake Chesterfield and shut my eyes. When I open them, the whole venue is silent.

I leave The Leadmill and check into my hotel. The promoter who I'm doing tonight's after show for has booked me into a Jury's Inn. I pass a gang of businessmen smoking vanilla cigarillos on my way in. The smell of cheap money. I order room service and lie on the big double bed until half an hour before we're due on stage.

When I get back to the dressing room, the band are working through the set list:

"I think it's a little bit long at the moment. It's too much to take in."

"It's only an hour and a half."

"I know, but anything longer doesn't work for us."

"True."

"I dunno why. Might be because our tunes are so short."

"An hour twenty is perfect when I'm watching a gig. I start getting bored after that."

"We could move *She Sings The Mourning* nearer the end."

"Yeah but that would ruin *Fear Machine*."

"Maybe we should just take *She's Coming Around* out of the set completely. That would sort everything."

"See how it goes tonight."

"Yeah."

"Yeah."

"Yeah."

We play a decent gig, and the crowd are lively. But it's almost like we had one eye on tomorrow's show in Manchester.

In the dressing room afterward, I pour a Jack Daniel's and knock it back neat, take a breath, grab my record bag and head into the night, toward the nearby after show venue, The Picture House Social.

Sheffield, 11/03/16

STRANGEWAYS HERE WE COME

I'm brought back into reality by the sound of a JCB digging up foundations outside the hotel. The sound mirrors exactly how my brain feels: wounded, like an open sore. I check the time: 11am. Two hours 'til the Manchester train. Plenty of time to recuperate.

I flick through the TV. *Sèance On A Wet Afternoon* is on. Richard Attenborough in crystalline eight-millimetre. I give up on getting a shower so I can see it through until the credits.

Last night's after show was strange. After the gig, I told the promoter to meet me outside the venue and we'd jump a taxi to his bar, where I'd DJ for a couple of hours. The venue itself was great; an old converted picture house with a couple of bars, a games room and café. Quite a few of the *lone wolf* sections of our fan base were there (separately), and wanted various things signing. There weren't many people dancing. I kept being pestered by a lad and a girl in matching black trench coats. The lad was a poet, he said, had read my books, and enjoyed them, "if not for the boring bits".

Near the end of the night, I was sat outside with the lad and his girlfriend, who he introduced as Jetta. There were a few more of them by now, kind of a gang, who all had the same kind of drawn, pompous look about them. The lad introduced himself as Isaac, and he said this with a little smirk as if there was some subtext I should have read into.

He was grilling me about writing, for the most part, and at one point he reached into his pocket and brought out a little black book. "These are my poems," he told me, and he began reading them aloud. Jetta and the others sat listening. Through the alcohol fug I struggled to gauge whether the poems were any good or not, but there were some real occult references in there. He laid it on thick. There was also a lot of Zodiac Killer-style numerology. Each poem had a chart on the page opposite and he explained to me how each letter in the poem corresponded with the chart and what it meant, and I kept nodding as if I understood what he was talking about.

I ended up getting dragged into a bedsit on the way home. There was some kind of party going on with Isaac and his crew of acolytes. I remember seeing a fat woman with blonde dreadlocks and facial studs sitting in a rocking chair. She was drinking from a Pot Noodle carcass. There were neon-pink fairy lights everywhere and those horrible cheap incense sticks burning, the type you buy in shops that sell bongs and Bob Marley posters. I ran away at some point, stumbled down a fire escape into the darkness.

One other thing on last night: as I walked the three miles back to the hotel, I stopped off at a kebab house. I ate sitting down at a bus stop outside the restaurant. I've just realised that I left my CD box there. It's gone. Took me about six years to build up that collection. Oh, well. RIP.

Sheffield, 12/03/16

STRANGEWAYS

"We'll be there tonight, weapons in hand" an anonymous text says on my phone. I'm stood on the platform at Sheffield station when a voice comes over the Tannoy announcing that all trains will be delayed by two hours. I haul my bags up the stone steps toward the café. I'll wait it out in there.

I arrive in Manchester four hours later than planned, but having slept clean through the journey, I feel rejuvenated.

The Albert Hall is beautiful. It's only recently opened as a live music venue and we've not played here before. Light pours in from its high stained glass windows. It's like something from Gotham City. Dramatic. You just know when it's going to be a good night. You can feel it.

All the mad ones are in tonight. The grafters, the huns, the hens, the space-cadets. Faces I know pop up in the dark then disappear again. Near the back I spot some of the Birkenhead contingent, and nearby, a lad who apparently runs an Arnold Schwarzenegger fan website.

Everything converges as we play, and rises to some hysterical state. It gets hot in there. The place is like a cauldron. Because of the high ceiling, our projection screen can be used at its maximum length. One photograph I've seen from that show looks as if we're playing on the surface of Saturn. We play a great version of *Put The Sun Back*, and in the extended section of *She's Got A Reason*, the stage seems to lift slightly from the floor.

As soon as we come off stage, people swarm into the dressing room. There's a small wall of polite security who don't stand a chance, and before long the room is rammed. A photographer we know, John

Badham is there, wide-eyed, sweating in a *Small Town Chase* T-shirt he's had made.

Our mates Keggo and Scott Judge appear. Blossoms pop back for a drink. Conrad and Dave from management. Andy Votel, who had been on DJ duties. Jane Weaver, all of The Sundowners, and a 16-year-old kid called Rory Wynne who's had a single out on Skeleton Key.

People are heaving in and out of the room, breezing past the doormen, who look to have given up for the night. More people pile in as fresh crates of lager are stacked against the wall. I don't remember much else except that it's half seven before I've made it to bed and all I can feel is the ground emitting a kind of reverse gravity, trying to pull me under.

Manchester, 12/03/16

DIARY OF FEELINGS (van excerpt)

"Albums should just document a period in time. That's it. Reflect the year, or two years or however long it took to write and record. I'm not sure they have to be any more than that. Sort of like a diary of feelings. And I think that's been lost, to an extent. D'you know what I'm getting at? Everything has to be *life-affirming* or *genre-defining* or *barrier-breaking* these days. And why is everyone trying to intellectualise music now? It's like the life's being sucked out of it."

"I know what you're saying, yeah. It's like if something's good then there's a forensic breakdown of the thing. The what's and why's. But a lot of art doesn't belong to the brain, does it? It's simple heart and soul a lot of the time. Attitude."

"And all this one-album-every-four years you get stuck on. Knock 'em out, you know the way Dylan or Leonard Cohen did. The Fall, even. They'd make albums, and if they were shit, they were shit. They'd just move on and make another. You know, we're not accountants, are we? We're trying to cultivate things that *live and breathe*, see what I mean?"

SMOKE

Steve Strange turned up before the show last night. Steve Strange is our booking agent. He stands five foot-three in his white lace-up trainers and laughs a hoarse laugh that you can hear from miles away. He was drinking Guinness from a plastic cup, telling us we should be proud and that the album turnaround is on "Lazarus levels".

I once saw Steve perform *Mustang Sally* at a huge party for an industry figure. He sang the shit out of it. Before him, Rick Astley had done Burt Bacharach numbers with a soft jazz band. For the final act, the jazz band took off their dinner jackets and bow-ties and Shane MacGowan got up and sang *Dirty Old Town* and *A Pair Of Brown Eyes*, and the crowd went nuts for it; Shane up there with one of those black hot-rod flame shirts on, no teeth and slicked back hair, blind drunk, barking his way through the tunes. It was unbelievable. If there was ever a true alchemy in practice, I witnessed it that night.

The story goes that they had to break Shane out of his hotel room three days later when he failed to respond to room maids wanting to wash the sheets. They had to kick the door in.

10am. I had my own room again last night. We're an hour or so outside of London, in Slough, and the view outside the window lives up to the stories I've heard. *Come friendly bombs, fall on Slough*.

Columbo is on the TV, the Johnny Cash episode, which is called *Swan Song*. In the episode, Cash's character plays a folk singer whose evangelist wife uses all his earnings to fund what she promises to be 'the greatest temple in the whole of America', for her church 'The Lost Souls Crusades'.

She threatens to reveal that Cash's character slept with an under age singer if he ever stopped performing. He eventually drugs her on a private jet flight and parachutes out before the plane crashes.

We hit the street in search of food before starting the journey to London. It's a pointless effort. We end up in Gregg's again, and swerve the vegetable pasties for the steak slice.

On the motorway, we talk about a documentary that James has seen called *Rubble Kings,* about gang warfare in the South Bronx in the mid-70s, and how the gangs eventually agreed on a truce. The following years gave way to the rise of hip hop, as the gangs focused their energies away from violence into music. Artists like Kool Herc and Afrika Bambaataa, who changed the name of his gang from The

Black Spades to the socially aware Zulu Nation.

In London, at the venue, we're standing under the *Close Encounters*-style ballroom ceiling of the Kentish Town Forum. The place is huge and we're the only ones in the main auditorium. We're talking about the cycle of music. How it's unbreakable. People proclaiming *the death of this and the death of that* and then being proved wrong at the last minute. We talk about how *Born To Run* and the resurrection of 50s music gave way to Ramones and the British punks.

Someone also remembers that our rehearsal room used to get so cold that we'd rent this huge industrial heater that looked like Del Shannon, and so we called it 'Del Shannon's head' for a whole winter.

Johnny Thieves arrives. Scott Judge and Keggo. Jay Redmo from The Viper Kings. My girlfriend, Aja is on a train from Lime Street and wants me to meet her at the tube station.

We head back to the hotel we're staying in, a cheap place outside Kentish Town called The Cornerhouse. I shower and watch TV on the bed until it's time to leave. There's a documentary on about a man who had a heart transplant, but soon after the operation he began having dreams and memories that belonged to somebody else. He traced the heart donor back and asked his family about his life. His own dreams "corresponded entirely", he said, with the donor's. "It's like he's in here, the pilot-light of his soul burning in mine".

We venture out into the night. We go to a place called Joe's Chicken Shack outside the gig venue. It's Aja's birthday in a couple of days so we decide to celebrate.

And it's a weird feeling. People are milling past on their way into the gig. They're coming in off the street, shaking my hand and congratulating me on the album. And I'm remembering how it feels again, to have been a part of creating something that people genuinely love. I'd almost forgotten.

London, 16/03/16

ONE DAY AFTER

Still no brain/soul activity. Getting home from London was a biblical journey. I'm sure most of us didn't sleep after the gig. At 7am a team of workers moved in to the hotel room above ours and decided to start laying a carpet. Cue relentless hammering that we thought might cave the Artex ceiling in altogether: *The Night Torn Mad With Footsteps.*

We eventually consoled one another all the way to Euston and forced ourselves to eat on the train, hoping we didn't bump into anyone from the previous night. The sweats, the shakes. The fear of sleep and of being awake.

That evening, Molloy texts to say, "Last night's after show was like Gomorrah." I can't argue with that. Our journey home was like *The Warriors*' fabled journey from The Bronx back to Coney Island. Or at least that's how it felt, minus the fighting. Still, it feels good to be back for a week or so. That is until Dave from management gets in touch to say we're booked in to *BBC Breakfast* television at 9 o'clock tomorrow morning for an interview and there's no ifs and buts about it, we're doing it.

Hoylake, 17/03/16

BBC BREAKFAST

It's a rough ride at 6am. Drifting onto the grey motorway like some long-distance meat-delivery truck. It's how much we stink. Of travel, of cheap hotel rooms, of concert venues.

The M62 scenery is the same for miles. Flooded fields. Helsby Hill on our right looks like Table Mountain. To the left, Stanlow oil refinery with its blinking spires of mystery and chemical clouds.

Our taxi is driven by Chris, a fella we know who's been following Status Quo and Hawkwind around for the best part of thirty years. The song on the cab stereo is *Hurry On Sundown.*

We chug into the BBC centre at Salford where we meet Dave from management. A quick coffee and a brush down in make-up by a girl called Honey. With the make-up on, I look a bit like a ventriloquist's doll. Or that I exist in black and white, and someone's filled the colours in on me.

The interview is swift and painless. We move out military style, as it's agreed sleep and rest are what we need. Out of the cab, I guide myself toward the front door like a homing missile.

19/03/16

LIVE AT PARR STREET

We're getting filmed today, at Parr Street Studios in Liverpool, where the new album was recorded. It's a pilot for a new Channel 4 series, so I'll have to make an effort. I'm looking through the pile of clothes I wore on tour that I haven't had a chance to wash yet. I dress quickly and slip out the front door.

While rehearsing between camera takes, a new song pops up, *Stormbreaker*, which comes from a riff Molloy plays in the extended section of *Fear Machine*. We make a rough recording and listen to a few playbacks in the control room, before packing away.

Onto the train, and back home. Tomorrow we leave early for a radio session in Scotland, before a Viola Beach memorial concert on Saturday.

Two days after that, a week-long trek across Europe. Paris, Amsterdam, Cologne, Hamburg, Berlin.

Liverpool, 30/03/16

WARRINGTON CONVERSATION

"Molloy found the Silver Apples third album on YouTube the other day."

"I didn't know they'd made a third?"

"Yeah. Weird covers of *Mustang Sally* with these huge analogue synths."

"Really?"

"Yeah. Mad what happened to them."

"What happened?"

"Have you seen that back cover, I think for the second album where there's a picture of a Pan Am plane that's blown up in the sky with them playing in front of it?"

"No."

"Well Pan Am sued them for that."

"Jesus."

"They impounded all the gear, everything."

"Everything?"

"All the patch oscillators, the synths, the drums. The main fella said every time he bought a new oscillator the drummer would buy a new snare or cymbal set. So there was a shitload of stuff. I think they still play actually."

"Yeah I heard they did Liverpool recently?"

"Not the drummer, it's only the synth player. I think he's gone, you know, in the head, like."

"Oh, is he on his own?"

"Yeah just him on the synths. Frazzled."

"You sure?"

"Think so."

Motorway, 02/04/16

REVIVAL (VIOLA BEACH TRIBUTE CONCERT)

Liam Fray from The Courteeners wants to make a coffee-table book of photographs he's taken over the years. Something for the fans, he tells me. There are loads of snaps on his phone. A lot are taken from the stage looking out into whatever arena he was playing that night. And maybe I could put some lyrics in there, and some chord boxes above the words, like *The Beatles Complete*, he says. You know, so kids can learn the songs sitting on the edge of their beds with a guitar.

The Kooks are in the corner of the room, doing strange vocal gymnastics before they're due to go on. They look isolated. Our mate Keggo is at the centre of things, audible to everybody, talking excitedly about 'Alaves 2001'. A band called The Strawberries are milling around, Blossoms, Dave McCabe, Conrad and Dave from management, Scott Judge and about three thousand people wearing Viola Beach T-shirts. The atmosphere is good; celebratory and not morbid, as I thought it might be.

We play four songs to close the night. It's rough and ready, as all the bands have shared equipment. As I said, it's a good atmosphere in Warrington Parr Hall. I can see some of the family members of Viola Beach dotted around the balcony. It's amazing that they've even made it here.

The stage itself is packed with the other bands, and a girl in jackboots who looks wired, throwing Altamont ‘69 shapes. She’s all over the side of the stage, gyrating, hula-hooping into people’s faces... *stay away from the brown acid.*

We jump a taxi around 3am. The dressing room is still full as we’re leaving, and there are heated conversations everywhere. It’s as if the night is just getting started. A man who looks like Albert Finney has the ear of three or four lads and I overhear snippets of their conversation: “I hit ’im with my best and he wouldn’t go down... no chance... who?... like in *Braveheart*... come and work for me on the fair, he said... no, I’m not injured, I’m just wearing a new pair of desert boots in. They’re ruthless on your heels, like... are you getting one? I’ll chip in...”

Next stop: Europe.

Warrington, 02/04/16

CHAPTER THREE

MEMORY TAPES (I)

Coming to America. Kings of the road. Deckard's arrest. Short cuts. Searching for Dracula's gaff. Death Valley and the quiet place. The ghost of electricity. Psycho truckers on speed.

KINGS OF THE ROAD

In 2003, we spent two weeks driving across the Bible Belt with the Kings Of Leon trailing us in another bus. It was early days for them, and they'd go on stage before us, believe it or not.

The Kings were all southern manners and polite applause at soundchecks. They were fun to be around for the most part, and you could tell that they were tough kids, but raised well. Their Oklahoma City style was worlds apart from our Northwest England bowlheads and corduroy jeans, though. They thought we looked like The Monkees.

They used to have this minder, a lad around the same age as them called Nacho. Nacho wore flares and cowboy boots, and had one of those haircuts where the back is outgrown and the sideburns look like they've been lopped off with Concorde wings. I hadn't seen a mullet like it since Billy-Ray Cyrus had done *Achy Breaky Heart* on *The Chart Show*.

They were obsessed with sex, too. They'd talk about it constantly. One time I walked past their bus to see them all sitting around smoking weed and casually watching a porno. I left them to it.

A few of the gigs were completely empty, the most notable being in Salt Lake City, Utah, which is a predominantly Mormon and Christian town. We wandered around for a short while, wondering where everyone was, until somebody pointed out that the place was deserted, "because it's fucking Sunday and everyone's in church".

In the rented chalets that circled around a swimming pool of green, stagnant water, we passed the post-gig witching hours stretched out in bed watching American TV. It was funny how many adverts you'd see for depression pills over there. There'd be this sad, dramatic thirty-second film, and then the short disclaimer at the end would say "side effects: may cause depression."

We sat in Caleb, the singer's, room for a while. They had this wooden homemade bong that was being passed around. It looked like something from the Civil-War era. Somebody changed the channel, and an old western came on, *The Searchers*, I think.

Caleb piped up: "Ah luurve John Wayne," he said. "I can put any John Wayne movie on and jus' sit there blubberin'." He went on: "Fuck it man, I'm a crier."

And then he'd load up the top of the homemade bong, and take another lungful.

SAKI

The Libertines came to see us in Japan. They were touring at the same time we were, and they introduced themselves by bundling through a stage door after we'd finished our first Tokyo gig. They'd seen the show, they said, and loved it. It's one of the only times we've ever met.

I struggled to take them in at first. The two lads who front the band are pretty tall. Taller than me even, and I'm pushing six-two without my shoes on. They were identically pale-faced, in the old rock'n'roll way I thought. *The ghost of electricity* and all that.

They wore ripped blue jeans and leather jackets each, with no shirts on underneath. They said they hadn't brought luggage with them, and had been up for days, tripping on something called 'Ice'. I thought they were a laugh. They picked up guitars and sang our songs back at us. They'd peddled the myth that in the early days, they'd sold *Dreaming Of You* to us in a New Brighton pub for fifty quid.

I thought that was a great lie, and most of us ran with it, until it started to become gospel, and we had to backtrack a little when people asked. Looking back, that part is even funnier.

In the dressing room, Pete, the singer, recommended I read Kerouac's *Lonesome Traveler*. There's a great chapter he said, where Jack spends six months in solitude as a fire watcher in a Canadian forest. I told him I'd try it. And then we all had a drink and a *good old knees-up*.

Eventually we dispersed into the suffocating neon thrum of Tokyo's late bars and cafés, steaming street noodle-bars that reminded me of *Blade Runner* and Deckard's arrest. There was a club there that lined up shots of Saki on the bar as we walked in. Then we really began to drink. There was quite a mob by that point. Us, along with some of that night's audience. Alan Wills and Joe Fearon. The Japanese record label. Our road crew, The Libertines road crew and The Libertines. And they set the pace.

One of our crew, a lad who'd been with us from the very beginning, thought that he could keep up with The Libertines on the Saki shots and took it as a challenge. But The Libertines were juiced up, fuelled by some superhuman Japanese nuke-drug, and all we had had was a severe dose of jetlag and the early symptoms of scurvy from the endless Big Macs we'd munched since arriving.

Most of us were back at the hotel by the time he stumbled through the door. His jacket was gone, and he had a Karate Kid style bandana around his head. His face had turned grey-green, the zombie hue.

He locked himself in the small hotel toilet. We'd knock on the door every now and then, just to check he was still breathing, but that seemed only to set the retching off again.

A couple of hours later he reappeared, half naked with a towel around his head. The bathroom was soaked, and there was sick everywhere, this strange black stuff that looked like crude oil. We'd found some weed by then, and found the whole thing more hilarious. We thought that the sick looked like the alien-infected goo from *The X-Files*, and that it could signal the end of the tour, quite possibly the world.

SHORT CUTS

Before it was taken over by a car mechanic, the unit below our rehearsal space was used exclusively as a 'spa and relaxation centre' by an organisation known as The Wirral Short Cut And Bald Club, which was basically one of those fetish/ swinger set-ups that you might have seen on a late night documentary on Channel 4 some time in the mid-90s.

One of the rules of joining the club was that your body had to be completely free of pubic hair. This was the foundation that the whole place was built on. Honestly. We looked it up.

It was run by Sue, a gravel-voiced woman who chain-smoked long cigarettes. Apparently her place was the continuation of an infamous local brothel called Norwegian Wood that was shut down just before the Open Golf Championship came to town. She still felt aggrieved by this, even while her new, unmarked and unnamed place was up and running.

You'd see all kinds of men pulling up outside. They'd be driving the kind of cars that had one door painted a different colour than the rest of the chassis. You know the type. Plumes of blue smoke spluttering from the exhaust. One day, as we were leaving rehearsals, a man with no eyebrows stuck his head out of the driver window asking for directions to "the spa", and we broke down, all of us on the pavement in hysterics, as he swiftly U-turned and sped back down the road.

Sue took me in once and showed me around the place. She was completely open about it. There was a huge black hot-tub in the corner of one room. An ugly, ceramic thing that was immaculately polished. Another room had a pool table in and a small bar with fairy lights pinned around oak wall panels.

You'd see Sue quite a bit in those days, and she'd always be affable and talkative, gift you a huge brown box full of condoms usually, that ended up in a pile in the corner of our room.

BUNNY-HOP

Ian McCulloch of Echo And The Bunnymen used to get taxis everywhere. Alan Wills told us he'd jumped a cab from London to Liverpool once, on the way home from some record company meeting, and charged the whole fare back to the label.

We were train kids. We took the train every day, as the buses over our side of the water are almost non-existent. There was a direct train link into Liverpool from where we lived on the coast. That was all we needed.

After signing our first record deal, and having some extra cash for the first time in our lives, getting the train started to seem like less of a necessity. We started hailing taxis more frequently, and from that period onwards, jumping a cab became known as *bunny-hopping.*

SUPER-APE

Lee Perry made music sound like the roots of a thousand-year-old rainforest tree. Like sludge and mud and buried bones at the bottom of the River Nile. Like ancient Pharaohs ploughing through a flooded wetland. As if the swamps and bayous had begun channelling spirits from the netherworld, and Perry was there with an old microphone, knee deep in rotten bark and cesspools, recording the whole thing.

We'd sit in that bedroom on the top floor of the house in a quiet street in the middle of a quiet suburb and through the course of a long night, be *transported.*

THE CASTLE

We wandered around LA for three hours once, looking for Bela Lugosi's old house, the house that Arthur Lee and Love had written the brunt of *Forever Changes* in. You can't miss it, people kept telling us. We'd seen it in pictures; Arthur Lee with his legs hanging down from the rubble of an outhouse in the overgrown gothic backyard. Bela in pyjamas, poring over newspapers, surrounded by oil portraits. And there we were in the searing heat, looking for *Dracula's gaff*, always within a hundred-metre radius of it. And people asking us, "Are you guys Irish? Are you guys Australian?" And us shaking our heads and mumbling something or other about The Beatles or Lennon, just to get it over with.

We never did find The Castle. Instead, we got sunburned and saw billboards and unmarked restaurants dotted down wide roads of Spanish bungalows.

We kept walking until we reached Sunset Boulevard, and a huge two-story record store called Amoeba, which if you've been to, will understand that Bela and The Castle were soon forgotten about.

PASS IT ON VIDEO SHOOT, DAY ONE

Death Valley, Nevada. Riding drowsily in the backseat of a hire car through dusty, unmarked roads with a film crew who'd flown in direct from Manchester a couple of days earlier. The surreality of the landscape; a border town full of stacked pickup trucks, stucco trailers and a jailhouse that was nothing more than a wooden cubicle. It looked like 'the box' from *Cool Hand Luke*, if you can picture that.

You see that old woman dancing at the end of the video? That's her house that we're in. She'd let us use it for the day. No questions. She told us she was a 'desert artist', and her front yard was full of decorated ram skulls, bleached bones, stuffed carcasses of prairie animals studded with cheap jewels and solar powered lights.

We sat with her and chatted and it seemed she was grateful for the company. At one point, she sat in a wicker chair with an old guitar and sang Hank Williams' *Long Gone Lonesome Blues* perfectly, with all the yodelling parts.

Near the end of the day I asked her about the skulls while we were stood out on the wooden porch:

"Oh my son Robert goes out and collects them for me. He never married. Something in him could never take to it. It's like he's in love with that thing out there, whatever you want to call it. The quiet place."

TRUCKIN'

We've had our fair share of lunatic bus drivers in the past. I can't remember one that didn't have a screw loose. We seem to have some magnetic pull toward each other.

There was Owen, the recently divorced born-again Christian, who ferried us across Europe one winter, on a bus with no heating. Owen wrote poetry; dark medieval stuff that he'd filled notebooks with. He'd recite it to us sometimes. In the quiet moments usually, when you couldn't be arsed listening.

There was Keith, the six foot-four bulldog-faced ex-bouncer who ate jellied eels from a Tupperware box. Keith hadn't liked us from the get-go. One time, he'd ended up barricading himself inside the bus, smashing all of the crockery, because, in his words, "We hadn't done any washing up since the tour began." The firm ended up having to send another driver up to Sunderland, or wherever we were playing that day.

And then there was Norm; the mustachioed redneck with the powerful bifocals and good ol' boy accent. Norm had been hired to drive us across America for a month in one of those wide berth single-decker buses with bunks. Norm had a disability as a result of having polio as a child. Or, as he put it himself, "a gimp leg."

It was common knowledge that most of the American truckers took speed in order to stay awake on the long hauls. A lot of them, including Norm, were toothless because they'd rub the speed into their gums. You couldn't tell whether they were on the speed or off it though; they were the same all the time: depressed, grouchy, ratty.

Norm would be on his CB a lot, giving it the *wilco* and *breaker breaker*, and he'd turn it on for us I think, as a show. And then later, when he thought we were all asleep, he'd put his foot down and hurtle down the great empty American highway. Joe Fearon peered through the curtain once, and swore that the speedometer hit one-twenty. For a ten-tonner, that's pretty fast. I had a lot of dreams about flying around that period.

Norm was from the Deep South, Virginia I think, and he still had a lot of the old ways about him. They were easy to spot. Not least when he stopped us from getting off the bus one day in Denver because there were some black kids walking – fairly innocuously – through the car park. We heard his muffled voice through the tinted windows of the bus, directing a volley of racist insults toward them. I swear this is true.

We passed through the Northern American states in a cruel, icy December. New York was first, followed by Boston. By the time we hit Chicago the snow was thick on the ground and you could see your breath in front of you. Gangs of men stood on street corners huddled around burning oil drums. Overhead, elevated trains rattled past on iron trestles. That's the thing about America. It's exactly how you've seen it in films.

We'd parked outside a KFC that night and had been speaking to a few of the local homeless community through the day. They'd knocked on the bus once or twice asking for a couple of dollars, or a cup of coffee, and we'd obliged. They all had these magnificent deep Illinois accents, like Muddy Waters. They were great to be around.

After the gig, we were winding down on the bus. We decided to get some food from the KFC opposite, and then go for a walk. "Don't forget the camera," somebody said.

We were shooting our own road movie around then, on one of those handheld digital things with the flip-out screens. America was full of bargain bins and thrift stores, and being so far away from home meant you could walk around in weird *Back To The Future II*-style jackets, trilbies and Davy Crockett hats. There's some great footage from that period.

Anyway, there was some leftover booze on the bus, so we decided to donate it to the homeless guys we'd been talking to. There were a couple of bottles of champagne, beer, a quart of whiskey and a bottle of Remy Martin. We had well-stocked riders on that tour, so there were drinks in abundance.

They were sat in the KFC, on a corner table near the window. We got talking again and they remembered us from earlier. They were a gang; they didn't look unhappy, and if they were they refused to let it show. There was a stoic pride in their togetherness, a refusal to be pitied. They'd been laughing between themselves before we arrived, blissfully unaware of anyone else in the restaurant.

You can see a video of it if you look it up. They weren't humbled by the gifts or anything, they just carried on with their own party. We asked them to say the name of the band into the camera, and one guy shouted, "Yeah! The Curry!"

At one point, I handed this fella a full bottle of Jack. Earlier, he'd performed a full monologue into the camera, sitting in the doorway of a department store. I saw him later and called out to him, but his eyes were gone. He looked clean through me, like we'd never met, and the bottle was nowhere to be seen.

Back on the bus, Norm wasn't pleased we'd been talking to the down-and-outs, not least because they were black. He'd tut and shake his head and say, "Well, don' say ah didn' warn yers."

That was our first tour of America, on which we supported Supergrass from New York through all the northern states and down to California, through Death Valley and the surrounding junk towns.

Death Valley was my favourite. It seemed to take days to pass through Nevada. We'd skirt through these ghost towns full of dust and scrapped cars; outdoor shacks that were used as jailhouses. It was like being an extra in *Badlands* or something, immersed in the full cinematic resplendence of the desert. This is probably my fondest memory of being in the States, along with being snowed in at a truck stop in Colorado for three days. But that's another story entirely.

One night, at a Motel in Amarillo, I wandered down from my hotel room into the bar. There was no show the following day, and Norm had met up with a couple of other truckers.

As I walked into the foyer, I saw Norm with a microphone, singing karaoke, limping around the small stage and singing at the top of his lungs, to the tune of *Stand By Your Man*:

'Sometimes it's hard being a freak/ craving the love/ of just one girl.'

A few of his friends were there, other truckers, who were laughing through their toothless gums and horseshoe moustaches at Norm, the tragic entertainer. He wasn't a bad singer and looked happy to be up there. But I couldn't help being struck by the pure sadness in him. The absolute solitude of his way of life, the estrangement from society. They stick together generally, long-haul drivers, have their own secret customs and communities up and down the highway. They're a closed shop.

I wanted to reach out to Norm, maybe talk to him, buy him a beer. But something stopped me. The fact that he was a demented racist probably had a lot to do with it. And I couldn't offer the olive branch. We'd passed that point days ago. We were near the end of the tour, and had ceased communication entirely.

Bus drivers and us, we're like chalk and cheese. We can't seem to find any middle ground. One of our longest serving guitar techs might have nailed it when he said one day, out of the blue, "I'm not surprised they all hate you, you've ruined every fucking bus you've ever been on."

Which was news to me.

CHAPTER FOUR

EUROPEAN TOUR AND BEYOND

Paul Simon's vampire fingers. Taxi Driver. Brighton Pier. Exit signs. Lucid dreaming. The Haarlem Hamster. Paris on the brink. On the move.

TRANS EUROPE EXPRESS

Before we cross the channel, a short detour by way of Brighton and The Concorde club. We haven't played Brighton in years, and the stop-gap is welcomed because we always seem to have a good gig there on the seafront. The purse for this show will also be enough to fund half of the European tour.

We set off for the journey at 9am. We're pretty muted, since everybody says they had a heavy weekend after the Viola Beach show. We go on in near silence, until the bus erupts into hysterics when somebody pulls a copied DVD of *Bula Quo* from their bag. *Bula Quo*, it turns out, is Status Quo's own feature length movie, set in Fiji. The blurb describes it as 'a cheeky crime caper with a musical twist.' We think that *Bula Quo* needs to be saved for a travel day, later in the week, when we've really lost our minds.

Instead, we flick through songs and talk music.

"Have you heard those live gigs when Butterfield and Al Kooper do two consecutive shows, but after the first concert Kooper does a load of drugs and ends up getting sectioned? They had to fly Steven Stills and Paul Simon and all these other stars last-minute to cover for him. They pull it off, too…"

"You know, Hal Blaine had three drum kits. Everyone wanted him to use the *Pet Sounds* kit on their sessions, so he'd just use that drum case and alternate between kits. Nobody knew..."

"You heard that new Black Mountain album?"

"That Tame Impala singer has got some guts… no guitars on the new one, just synths..."

Outside an A-road cafe is where we notice the flat tyre. Big John pulls in and inspects the damage. He says we're lucky it didn't happen on the motorway or it could've flipped the van.

Everybody has a go at getting the wheel off. The jack doesn't work, and it takes a couple of us to even get the wheel wrench to move. It almost snaps as I put my body weight on it.

I've no idea where the fuck we are, but I see Big John crossing the road to a warehouse with a sign that reads 'Leatherhead Van and Truck Limited.' He comes back trailed by a local mechanic. His face is black with oil and he works for half an hour or so on the tyre. John slips him twenty quid for his troubles. It's a welcome help and it's saved us a lot of time.

After pulling in to Brighton promenade we head toward the pier.

There are bright signs everywhere as we approach the crowded jetty: 'We Sell Neon'. 'Brighton Rock'. 'Fish n' Liquor'. 'Horatio's Bar', then somebody points to a house and says, "Isn't that where Nick Cave lives?"

There are two piers in Brighton. A newer, working pier, and one from the Victorian era. The old pier caught fire some time in the early noughties. I remember, because someone posted the *Brighton Argus* front page to me with a photograph of the inferno and news report. I've no idea who it was. Anyway, the rumour is that the owners of the newer pier burned the old one down on purpose. That's what I'm told, anyway. I'd like to think it's true. It's a good story.

She Drew The Gun play before us tonight. Their song *Poem* has been getting some good airtime recently, and rightly so. In fact, all of their songs hit the mark. Sam isn't with us to do the projections for the gig, but it's a good show anyway. He'll meet us in Paris tomorrow.

There's a good view of the sea from where I am on the stage. The sky is darkening now, and the blur of the pier lights are blinking through the dusk. I think of the old pier out there, the burnt out skeletal frame of itself, not moving or wavering against the weight of the tide. It's as if it's been in that state forever, the new pier forced to watch it sit there, like some decaying premonition of itself.

Brighton, 05/04/16

PARIS

Early dart at 8am. for the Chunnel. We're late and have to speed into the car park to make it. Only thing is, we've got the times mixed up and are actually an hour early, so we decide to go for something to eat.

After the short train journey, we roll out of the Eurostar and onto foreign soil. It's the first time I've been away for months, and it feels great to get off the island. I've been to France countless times but I'd never noticed these beautiful odd electricity pylons stretching across the green fields near the tunnel entrance. The pylons look like men in stocks, waiting for the guillotine.

Tim from The Sundowners and Chris Taylor follow us in another van with the instruments. They're on tech/sound duties, and are pulling off the near impossible on this tour with just the two of them taking care of the whole backline.

We drift past the Stade de France and ghost slowly into the city. Tonight's gig had to be rescheduled, as it was originally booked into the Bataclan club, where the recent terrorist attacks took place. You can still feel the atmosphere on the streets. Paris seems like a city on the brink. There's a market closing down as we crawl along in traffic, and people are milling about the street, walking in the road. There are women on the pavement holding babies. Some of them want to wash windscreens for a handful of coins. Others hold placards marked with scribbled words I can't read. There's a sense of tension everywhere. Maybe that's just coming from me.

This is the place where years ago we used to run up and down Montmarte, creased with laughter, diving in and out of sex shops, hanging around outside the Moulin Rouge. We'd wander up to Notre Dame and take in the gothic architecture and duck into tiny side street bars. It was completely carefree. Things seem eerily different now, as if something's about to give.

Backstage at Le Trianon, we share an outdoor balcony with Blossoms, who will be joining us on the tour. We have a drink, and they are in high spirits for the forthcoming couple of weeks. A photographer called Alain takes photos of us as we mill about the dressing rooms, talking, playing table football.

During the gig, I have a direct view to the two main exit doors from my position on the stage. I'd be lying if I said my eyes don't dart nervously over to each one over the course of the show. I feel relieved when it's over. The same, however, can't be said for the audience, who don't budge once. It's almost like some defiant celebration. Considering the events of the past few months, it's hard not to admire that.

Paris, 06/04/16

FLATLANDS

We pulled in late last night to a motorway hotel on the border of France and Holland. The place looked like one of those fireproof buildings people use to store furniture in. The front door was a metal shutter. You had to type a code into an electronic panel to get in. Once the shutter had gone up, you had to type a booking code into another panel. Nobody worked there. There wasn't even a front desk. Of course, the code didn't work, and seven of us were stood in the tiny doorway for two hours while Big John had to re-book the whole thing online. That was at 2am.

Today is a travel day. I get up and survey the area surrounding the hotel from my window. It's quiet. There are shops and cafés I think, but nobody seems to be here. Even the motorway on the other side of the hotel is desolate.

I wander around in a half-daze with my bag over my shoulder, a heavy travel hold-all trailing me with my coat draped over the handle. There isn't a soul in sight. There are warehouses around me, what seems to be a Laser Quest, a kids soft-play centre and a huge American style diner called Maxwell's. Weird sanitised buildings surrounded by neat pavements of grass. It's like everybody fled from here before it was completed. It's dead.

Outside Maxwell's, French-speaking workers tell me in broken English that the place is still being built and doesn't open for another month. I nod and haul my things back through the car park.

I end up seeing James and Ian in a pizza joint, which is bursting with people at 10am. I sit down and we order coffees and a slice of pepperoni. The waiter tells us we can only order a full pizza, and opens his arms to demonstrate. He darts back later with an espresso, and I explain in the clearest possible way that I'm after a cappuccino. I open my arms to demonstrate.

After some back and forth chat, we end up with three Irish coffees in tall glasses with about four inches of whipped cream floating at the top and curly straws jutting out of the froth. They're enormous. There must be about three shots of whiskey in there. I finish mine, and feel drunk instantly.

We meet up with the rest of the band outside a nearby Burger King. As we're waiting for the van to swing around, somebody locks the main exit gate, so we have to walk through the drive-thru to get out. As we walk past the intercom, an automated voice in Flemish asks us what meal we want.

In the van, somebody pulls out a *Lethal Weapon* box set and suggests we watch them all (backwards) to help pass the journey. It goes to a vote; watching the *Lethal Weapon* quadrilogy (backwards) beats *The Lost Boys* by three votes to two, then is abandoned before we get past the opening scene.

Because of traffic, the drive to Haarlem, outside Amsterdam, ends up taking eight hours instead of four, and we're glad to eventually reach the hotel.

As there is no gig tonight, everyone meets in a bar around the corner from the hotel to watch Liverpool play Borussia Dortmund. The bartender recognises us, and keeps playing these weird thirty-second mash-ups of *Dreaming Of You* and *In The Morning* through the wall speakers.

We get drunk, dirt drunk, and the night ends in a couple of us getting chased by irate bicycle owners. God knows why. Nobody can seem to remember.

I get back to my room and fall asleep. I dream that I'm on a bike myself, and I'm getting chased, though the bike is attached to a car trailer. You know, the type they use in films to make it look like the actors are driving. One of those. And I think it's a gang of old schoolteachers who are chasing me up this winding mountain road.

I kept looking back to get a glimpse of them, but all I could see was the whole of Europe below, engulfed in a great burning sea, the land underneath being broiled like a blue lobster.

Haarlem, 07/04/16

MOTORWAY

Midway across a stretch of asphalt somewhere between Antwerp and Amsterdam, we're listening to an early Frank Sinatra recording of *Nature Boy*. The whole arrangement is just voices. Voices where instruments should be. High, ghostly voices that sound like they're underwater, and then Sinatra, whispering over those voices, gliding himself over the surface.

The van is dark and everybody is straining against their eyelids. Outside, the traffic is being funnelled into one lane. An identical van to ours has crashed on the embankment at the side of the motorway. It's eerie as we pass. It's like I'm the only person who sees it. And then someone says through the smoke and the mist that seeps through the driver window... *how far are we?...* and then the words, from the cheap speakers of the transit van... *the greatest thing you'll ever learn is just to love... and be loved in return...*

DUFFY PLAYLIST/ AMSTERDAM ROUTE

Pink Floyd – *One Of These Days*
Goblin – *Profondo Rosso*
Neu! – *Isi*
Kraftwerk – *Autobahn*
Mulatu Astatke – *Masengo*
The Move – *Blackberry Way*
The Soundcarriers – *Last Broadcast*
Angelo Badalamenti – *Laura Palmer's Theme*
John Carpenter – *Escape From New York*

Motorway, 08/04/16

THE MILK BAR

Half of our hometown must be here. I'm serious. The place is full of people I know. I'm peering through the stage curtain looking out at the sea of bodies. Blossoms have just finished their set and I'm stood here picking out faces I recognise. There are lads here I play football with. A few who are in bands. Old school friends. Everyone seems relaxed, as they've been in and out of Amsterdam coffee shops all day.

I'm still nursing a hangover from the night in Haarlem. Apparently, our mate Scott Judge ate a burger that was so bad it looked like a deep-fried hamster. It's been christened *The Haarlem Hamster*, and even gets a dedication during the gig.

On my way to the bar, I overhear someone say they are out later to "score a hat-trick of brass" which I won't bother to explain. A lad I know who's standing in the audience texts me to say, "There's a lad and a girl out here who've just necked a bag of Mexican mushrooms, so those projections of yours are going to send him to the loony bin..."

I've always seen this part of the city as a kind of prisoner to itself. At night, anyway. I get the impression people aren't sure who's paying to see what any more. It's almost as if the tourists have become the performers and the hookers and dealers are the ones who are condemned to watch them. It's gone full circle, like they are all stuck here.

I watch people spill out of the main exit and disappear into the night. They wander out toward the red neon, the dark network of veins that constitute *Singel, de Pijp* and *Walletjes.*

Amsterdam, 08/04/16

COLOGNE

We meet in the hotel foyer late, and miss the hotel breakfast, so the first service station we stop off at I order an enormous Bratwurst in curry sauce with fried potatoes. It does a good job. Germany feels alright.

After that it's plain sailing to Cologne. We've got The Black Keys and the Traveling Wilburys on the stereo. Good-time, driving music. It's what you need on the road, otherwise you start dragging your heels.

Next to the venue is a huge flyover, a disused railway line, and then around the corner a massive greenhouse full of palm trees and exotic plants. It looks like some kind of GM testing centre. *The Island Of Dr Moreau*.

There doesn't seem to be much else around here so we slip inside the dark venue and into the tiny dressing room where there are three chairs between seven of us, and one toilet. I remember an important lesson: the thing to do in a situation like this is drink through it, slowly.

I'm always surprised by how easy it is to lose yourself on tour. The sense of yourself, who you are. It can disappear within days of being on the road. And so you fall into acting out characters and doing impressions and drinking bottles of lager with your breakfast. There's no way around it.

We wander aimlessly around the Lux area for two hours or so. There is talk of going to see a cathedral somewhere, but no-one can be arsed enough to look for directions. It's one of those days when you have to admit defeat. It's the only option. A good record store that we've been to before (Schallhandel) is closed, and we retreat back to the club after a while to eat Haribo and smoke and drink warm Becks. And it reminds me of the last time we were in Cologne some years ago, hung over and coming down off whatever it was and we all bought cigars and lay on one king-sized hotel bed and watched *Taxi Driver* until it was time to go on stage

Cologne 09/04/16

TRANSIENT HOTEL

Stopovers for ghosts. Hotels at the city limits, borderlines and no wi-fi zones. Motorway graveyards for the freighters, the long-haulers, and us. We attract puzzled looks from people as we mill about these places in sunglasses and trapper hats, but I don't feel at odds with them in any way. Their nonchalance is somehow comforting. You see them dotted about the hotel, drinking, chain-smoking, staring out at the highway. And here we are in these grey and white concrete slabs with identical portholes, bored out of our minds. We begin pointing out every symbol of depression, like some twisted game of I-Spy.

One of us goes a step further, and decides to document it with photographs. We stop at every grotty corner and bus stop in the area. We've reached the point where cabin fever has kicked in, and are walking around either in hysterics, or complete silence. We must look strange to anyone who isn't part of the group. The photo shoot continues. The resulting book of pictures will, after some ideas are thrown around, be called *Shithole*.

LUCID DREAM

Remember that winter when we first met and the roads were quilted in muddy slush and the buses were freezing on the top deck when we rode into town? Four, five nights a week in the bars and pubs and falling over and shivering all night in the box room of your mum's house.

You used to cut your own hair in those days. You had a go at mine too, with a pair of kitchen scissors, and I had to wear a hat for two weeks 'til it grew back. But how cold it was. It was all we talked about. The cold, the cold in our bones. The crisp snow down Penny Lane and the pigeons shivering on the boarded up windowsills of The Punch Bowl. The endless journeys home after being up all night in some unknown flat, forcing chow mein down our throats on the corner of your road so we didn't die of starvation.

I never wanted anyone as much as I did then. I can almost see you in front of me, the image of you clear and crystalline. But then the image begins to dissolve and I can hear somebody knocking at the hotel room door shouting, "TEN MINUTES 'TIL WE LEAVE."

HAMBURG

Soundtracking our journey into the port city is Cypress Hill's *Temple Of Boom,* Black Sabbath's *Paranoid*, Tav Falco's Panther Burns' *Behind The Magnolia Curtain*, and an album I'd never heard before called *The Hot Spot*, which is a soundtrack to the film of the same name, and features John Lee Hooker, Miles Davis and Taj Mahal all in the same band.

After a long drive, we pull in at a hotel on the peripheries of the city.

The hotel is right next to a petrol station, and there is the strong smell of gasoline everywhere. Still, everyone has their own room tonight. We dump bags, lock doors and head into town.

It's sunny here in Hamburg. A welcome respite after the brutal landscape of Cologne. The streets are full of colourful graffiti murals. The Knust, where we'll play, sits just behind the fairground. We take a wander over there after soundcheck, and then into a great little bar with a pool table in, where we spend the remainder of the day.

Blossoms play a blinder tonight, but warn us that, "there are a few hicks from your neck of the woods in the audience," and sure enough they're at the front, shouting out for singles and "Play something we fucking know!" but generally they do whip up a kind of storm and end up jarring the local crowd into life.

Afterwards, in the shared dressing room, we're having a drink. Blossoms are hot for the Reeperbahn and the feeling is that things will move in that direction. I carry on drinking whiskey so as to dream my way through the night. The last couple of days have caught up with me.

In the morning, I wake up on top of the quilt. The night is a blur, though I do remember bumping into a couple of lads from near where I live. They'd bunked over last minute they said, just to see us, and had spent all their money in the day. They weren't sure if they had enough to make it home, and thought they might have to do a stint on the Reeperbahn themselves, just to make the funds back.

Hamburg 10/04/16

SHOWTIME/ THREE WAY CONVERSATION

"...you know, the Showtime ice cream vans?"

"Course, yeah. They used to be everywhere."

"Well, there's this massive warehouse in Birkenhead where they are all stored. My dad used to take us when we were kids."

"Why?"

"Honestly, I don't know. He worked on one for a bit. I did a few shifts with him."

"He claims he sold Prince a 99er after a concert in Wembley."

"That's brilliant. What a myth."

"I worked the side-bit for a while, the soft drinks section. He had Panda Cola at a massively inflated price and it sold fuck all."

"There's something weird about the ice cream scene though, isn't there? Some underworld connection? Has to be."

"Undoubtedly, yeah."

"I was doing a video for Serpent Power and I was trying to film my granddad in an alien suit, buying a Calippo from a Showtime van. But the fella behind the counter, he wasn't having it. He said he didn't want his face to be on camera. He drove off after that."

Autobahn, 11/04/16

BERLIN

Things get blurry from here on in. It's a culmination of things. The hotel we're in, The Pankow, doesn't even make the map of Berlin, it's that far out of the city limits. It's a no wi-fi zone too, but that doesn't bother me at this stage. I'm on auto-pilot.

Duffy has pulled his shoulder out of place, so is sitting in an armchair in his room, dosed up on painkillers.

The rest of us spend a full afternoon in the Pankow bar. After that, a taxi ride and the unparalleled sights of the Pariser Platz and The Brandenburg Gate. It really is a beautiful area. We meet Conrad from management and have a huge meal together, all of us, and then head into town.

The next morning it rains while we eat our breakfast on the street. Someone has picked up something called a "Biffy", which looks like a sausage roll inside a cake. We're daring each other to have a taste.

The Lido club, where we're playing tonight, is a perfectly square paisley wallpapered room that, according to Chris on the sound desk, is "a nightmare to get a grip of." Despite the sound issues, the place is sold out, packed full.

While we play, I see Anton Newcombe in the audience. I recognise the mutton chop sideburns. He's nodding along in a cravat and wraparound shades. He mentions later that the sound in Europe is so geared to eurodisco and techno DJs that your sound guy really has to be prepared for that level of sub-bass. He said it was deafening at times.

Later, we spill out into Berlin with some local fans. We're roaming the streets with a manic thirst for something. No one seems to know where to go on a Tuesday night in this district, so we buy a couple of beers each from a newsagent and drink as we walk.

On the corner of an unlit road, we stumble down a set of steps and onto a black and white checkerboard tiled floor. The dungeon bar we're in has songs playing at half speed. The one playing is ABBA's *SOS*, and it sounds like some Quaalude nightmare. Still, it kind of fits. Everybody in here is pretty drunk. A couple at the back wall stand straight backed, staring blankly out. It's as if they've modeled their look on the Moors Murderers. Another girl in bumble bee tights runs around the dance floor holding a pair of sparklers, sucking on a sugar dummy.

At some point, Dion's *King Of The New York Streets* comes blaring through the speakers. The next thing I remember is being on a street corner in a huddle with everyone singing the same Dion song, local residents hanging out of windows shouting insults to us in broken English.

The night ends with us drinking around a table outside the Pankow, watching the morning trams hum quietly down rows of identical concrete apartment buildings in the rising light.

Well I'm on the plane writing this, almost dreaming through my eyelids. The fact that the tour is over makes me feel about a stone lighter. Honestly. I feel like I'm floating.

We're sitting in front of a gang of Borussia Dortmund supporters who are on their way to Liverpool, and the atmosphere is good, as if we're being sung home by the fans. I begin recognising patterns of illuminated streets below, labyrinth roads and dark canals. As we descend further, I swear I can see Anfield in a halo of light.

Next, we're in the taxi from Liverpool airport, talking about how good it'll be to have a week off, when a piece of good news lands: Dave from management texts to say we've landed a spec on the TV show *Later... With Jools Holland*, and that we might be on the same night as Paul Simon. Filming begins in two days.

Liverpool, 13/04/16

THE RETURN

Noises between noises, pauses
and then noises again

hello walls

hello   *hello*

the faint train whistle of tinnitus
stood in bedroom doorway watching silhouette of
her wrapped in a curlew
quilt

my voice then
... and the land I've seen, you
wouldn't believe all of the great
land I've seen out there love
I think God mighta made this
Earth after all
and even daft sunburned people
in sandals and socks
on Berlin trams
and Amsterdam canals
are his creation...

can *anybody* hear me?

I creak back downstairs
to the night kitchen
mold spores on teabags
busted fridge-bulb   milk
on the turn
(she doesn't drink tea)
I run my palms over the cold
walls
through the
darkness
trying to remember

LATER...

Paul Simon is standing in the middle of the dark TV studio, illuminated by a single spotlight. There are about 15 or so people in the huge hangar that hides off a back road in Maidstone, Kent. A camera crew, a couple of technicians and three or four of Paul Simon's assistants. Earlier, from outside, we'd heard the faint strains of a guitar chord as we were headed back toward the dressing room. I knew instantly that it was him. You get to know a person's tone when you've listened to it for a period of time.

Anyway, he's standing there with a guitar around his neck. I'm watching him from behind my own keyboards. If you've seen the show, you'll know that different bands are set up around the room in a vague circle. They've put Simon at the dead centre of it all. Everything is silent except for the hum of these giant coolers on the ceiling.

The first thing I notice is that he looks old. His hands are almost bird-like, the fingernails on his right claw-picking hand are long, like the vampire in that movie *Fright Night*. The baseball cap has gone, revealing a thin forelock of silver hair that runs down his skull. He's still sharp though. He brushes his fingers across the guitar strings and the room seems to drop into a heavier state of silence. Then he launches into it... *hello darkness my old friend*... and before I know it I've floated down from the ceiling and Simon and his entourage have left. These enormous bars of pink and blue neon lights are popping into life all around us and the whole studio looks like Superman's Kryptonite cave.

Kent, 15/04/16

LATER... #2

Paul Simon was one of the voices of my childhood. I remember dancing around to the video of *You Can Call Me Al* in our front room, the video where Chevy Chase mimes the words in a white tuxedo jacket and jeans.

I became obsessed with Paul Simon later on in my 20s when I went back to the Simon and Garfunkel stuff and then onto the solo albums. I bought albums, songbooks, the lot.

After the first camera rehearsal yesterday, we went to a local Nepalese restaurant. During the meal, we were laughing about something called 'Rupert Pupkin hour'. Rupert Pupkin was the obsessive fan-comedian played by Robert De Niro in the film *The King Of Comedy*. The character would go into these long flights of fancy about hitting the big time and becoming friends with his hero Jerry Lewis.

Everyone has experienced a Rupert Pupkin hour. It usually happens somewhere near dawn, between waking and sleeping, when the mind wanders.

It's admitted that last night, most of us had dreamed up their own Pupkin hour scenario around Paul Simon. In mine, we talked for a while, exchanged hats and he ended up asking me to play some Wurlitzer on his world tour.

After the final camera rehearsal of *Chasing The Tail Of A Dream*, Duffy's own Pupkin hour becomes a reality, when Paul Simon hops over a couple of monitors, leans in to him and says, "Hey… just wanted to say I love the way your bass line weaves in and out of the chords. Great playing."

London, 15/04/16

HEAR NO EVIL

Dion's Phil Spector-produced album... Frank Frazetta and Boris Vallejo's fantasy landscapes... Michael Moorcock and the world of comics that followed... *Revolutionary Road* and Tom Wood and photographs of New Brighton in the 90s... Vangelis... Billie Holiday… Steve Marriott… Afrika Bambaataa... ribbon microphones... Prophet synthesizers... Don Delillo's *Underworld*... *Four Sail* followed by Buster Keaton's stunts... Jane Weaver… Atlantic City's pre-war mob... Norma Jean and the Kennedys... Gerald Gardner's witchcraft revolution... Evel Knievel and then the Montauk Monster... Springheel Jack... *Dark Star* and Ludwig snares... The Black Ark... Shadow Morton into *The Larry Sanders Show*... Ronnie Spector... Spector vs Rector… *The Magical World Of The Strands* and this endless hunger to just dig and burrow and consume and read, listen, and *absorb*.

MILLION EYES

We're in a studio space in a loft on Vulcan Street, near the Bootle docks. The end of the road opens out to a full view of the Mersey. I'm watching it from an upstairs window. It's been a hot day today and the river is shimmering. Freightliners creek drowsily into port, huge hulks of steel carrying iron containers, stacked like Lego.

We're here to shoot the video for *Million Eyes*, the fourth single from the new album. All of our instruments are set up in a huge white room with a projector near the back. Opposite, there is a small bar with a pair of deer antlers screwed into a parapet. High up, a bricked up window houses an old super-eight camera on a stand with a pair of mannequin legs dangling down from the middle tripod.

It's 8 o'clock in the evening now. Video shoots are generally easy when there's a concept in place; all you have to do is sit there and mime. We've played this song on long English and European tours, so it's ingrained into our brains, and there isn't much concentration needed.

We use Sam's projections and stand directly in front of the light beam. Behind where we're stood, a screen digests the colours and reflects our silhouettes back at us.

Back outside, between takes, I look at the dockland and try to imagine how it will look with a huge stage in the middle of it, and our projections beaming bright over the river.

Three approaching gigs: one in Stoke, one in London. 26 days until we headline the Sound City festival, two minutes down the road from here.

Liverpool, 03/05/16

ON THE BUSES/ STOKE

Scott Judge is driving today. Big John will meet us tomorrow, as he is at the funeral of a well-loved Liverpool musician, Kris Ealey, who died suddenly in his sleep not two days ago. We knew Kris when we played gigs with Tramp Attack in the early days of the band, and he was known by everyone around town. He was only 38.

It's hot in the van and the thought of staying over and DJing tonight is adding to the discomfort. Tonight's gig is a warm-up for the forthcoming slot at the Sound City festival. There's also a midweek gig in London for competition winners. It's about getting match-fit again. It's been over a month since Berlin.

In Stoke, we soundcheck and I dive out of the venue to check into my hotel. It's above a pub, and I have to stand there rattling the door for half an hour while a Rottweiler stares at me from behind the glass. A woman with shorn blonde hair eventually lets me in. She's wearing these odd-coloured breeches over a striped hoteliers uniform. She wants to hurry me into my room, as something is happening behind her in the scruffy yard they're using as a beer garden. There's a smell like a bonfire and murmured voices of men and women drunkenly arguing.

On the second floor, the room is nice enough. Clean sheets. Tea and coffee. I lie on the bed for a while and watch TV before I'll go back up to The Sugarmill, where tonight's gig is. I'm trying to flick between channels but the TV is stuck on one station that's showing reruns of *On The Buses.* One of the speakers is broken, and the canned laughter from the show sounds like hoarse distress signals from purgatory. The whole place is stifling. I try to let some air in but the windows are painted shut.

After the gig, I DJ alongside a man with a perm and some kind of soul glow finish sprayed onto it. He plays horrific indie songs that melt into each other seamlessly. I play some northern soul and that seems to go down well for a while.

Around 3 o'clock, I say my goodbyes to the permed compere and stumble up a set of metal stairs to the promoter's office. I knock and he motions me in.

He's sat behind a desk, a bald man in his sixties with a black hoodie on and skater pumps popping out the end of the desk. He has a stammer but that doesn't stop him launching into a half-hour monologue describing how hard it used to be "bouncing the doors in Blackpool". Still, he hands me an envelope stuffed full of twenties so I can't complain. It's all there too, which is a rarity for the DJ circuit. There's usually an argument or two involved. I amble back to the hotel with one hand clasped tight over my front pocket, where the money is.

In the morning, I run a bath and listen to *In The Wee Small Hours* by Frank Sinatra, and wait until it's time to leave for the train.

Oh, and Prince died last month. So far, that's him, Bowie, George Martin, Lemmy and Glenn Frey. What a strange year.

Stoke-on-Trent 20/05/16

LONDON-BOUND. THREE-WAY CONVERSATION

"I was watching videos for hours last night about that Planet X."

"Oh, right."

"It throws up all sorts of questions you know."

"Like what?"

"Just stuff relating to things that are mysteries. Like the pyramids for instance. If extra-terrestrials built them."

"Aliens didn't build the pyramids, did they fuck."

"They did!"

"You can't say that as if it was a fact."

"Well, I believe it."

"The world is boring and people need something to fill their imaginations with. *That's* a fact."

"You can't discount it though."

"If there were two buttons in front of you – one yes and one no – and you were asked if aliens built the pyramids, and your life depended on getting the answer right, I guarantee you'd say no."

"You're wrong."

"Alright then."

"A lot of the initial information was received by shamans on DMT trips."

"Well, I can sort of believe that."

"Well, why one and not the other?"

"I just think the scariest thing a person can think is that we're hurtling through space alone, and no-one gives a shit. So theories get invented."

"You know about Michael Aquino and all of the MK mind control stuff in the American military?"

"Some, not a lot."

"Well, he was a Satanist who founded his own temple, the Temple Of Set."

"Yeah I heard about that."

"And he was head of psychological warfare for the US army. Can you believe that?"

"Really?"

"Yeah he was on Ricki Lake."

"Course he was."

"Have you been to the club where tonight's gig is?"

"No."

"Looks like some weird cross between Stringfellows circa 1993 and the nightclub in *Basic Instinct."*

"Neon smut."

"Like if Bon Jovi's hair designed a building."

Motorway, 26/05/16

COMPETITION WINNERS

"It's more like the set of *Robot Wars* than Stringfellows." someone says as we walk past the security, through passport and retina-scan booths that give everything a *Total Recall* feel. Not least the neon pink lights and huge, odd sex symbol effigies that hang from the ceiling in the main hall.

Tonight's gig, in the Kingston district of London, is the fulfilment of a record company deal where early copies of the album were sold along with a ticket. It's no bad thing; a show is a show and we're finding we've been enjoying this live set probably more than any we ever have. The songs on this album are more geared to live shows, and more fun to play. We'd have to soundcheck for hours on some previous albums. Balancing the harmonies, picking out the right acoustics. This one feels like we can just roll up and plug in, which is like a new lease of life.

Danny Roberts is on guitar tech duties today. We know Danny from the Zanzibar scene that we became a part of, which included bands like Tramp Attack, The Bandits, The Stands, The Zutons and Danny's band, The Hokum Clones.

His band were an acoustic duo that played delta music from about the 1920s onwards. Ragtime, folk, murder ballads, country blues, bluegrass.

The Hokum Clones were Danny and Robbie Stevenson, and when they played Robert Johnson's *If I Had Possession Over Judgement Day*, the walls would shake.

Post-gig in the venue, we amble about in the club that has re-opened as a student disco night. I talk to a pair of twins who own a "vintage map shop" somewhere near Kensington and even more strangely, a BMX gang who've followed our career through the soundtracks of skate videos. Which I hadn't been aware of.

London, 26/05/16

CHAPTER FIVE

FESTIVAL SEASON

Power-out at the homecoming. Stone Roses support.
Hallucinations in Zagreb. The wall of death.
Fear and loathing in Brum.
Stolen bags in Barcelona.

POWER-OUT

Here I am waiting by the side of the stage midway through a set at Liverpool Sound City. The festival sits at the side of the River Mersey at the Bramley-Moore dock. There are the ghosts of the old working port everywhere you look; granite clock towers and empty warehouses. Steel moorings jut out of the harbour side, and beyond those, the grand vista of Liverpool Bay and the Irish Sea.

We arrive late, around 8pm, and the bright sun has begun to shallow. We mooch about backstage, do the odd interview, nurse a beer or two. It's a headline gig but the mood is relaxed – we've done enough touring this year to feel confident.

About 15 minutes into the performance, during the instrumental break of *Connector*, the power cuts on stage. A flash of pure darkness and then a silence. Up until then we'd been flying. Supercharged. It's a shame really, as there was a sense of something building. Still, the audience stay put in the pitch-black dock and sing our songs among themselves, almost willing the dud generator back into life. It's quite a thing to see, this dark mass of people swaying like an ocean, flanked by the silver river and these huge silhouetted container cranes behind it all. Pockets of mobile phone lights popping up like will-o'-the-wisp. It's turned into some strange inverted victory.

Earlier in the day, we'd soundchecked under a clear blue sky. The weather couldn't have been better. The dock was quiet then, in the bright morning, dust settling on the previous night's celebrations. Huge yellow JCB diggers collected rubbish into piles while uniformed barmaids watched from faraway benches as we picked our way through the set. Some of us even received texts from relatives who could hear us way over the Mersey in New Brighton. We were the only sound on the river, save for the odd passing freight container fog-horning its way out of port.

In front of me, I can see engineers and technicians running frantically to and from the stage. A front loader hauls the huge wounded generator toward a substation at the edge of a dock. It looks like a patient being rushed into accident and emergency. A pair of jump leads are found to try and resuscitate the thing and resume the gig. The place is in a panic.

Ten minutes later the power surges back into life. A bright ricochet of light pings back from the audience and the sky turns from tar black into a kind of haunted indigo, and suddenly we're back on stage, ploughing through the set. We finish to a humbling applause and it feels like something's been pulled back from the brink.

It's my birthday as of midnight tonight. I come off stage and am still annoyed by the power cut. I see Aja and a few mates walking in my direction singing me happy birthday. I'm not in such a good mood though, so I skulk off behind one of the cabins for a smoke, feeling bad about it all.

People are milling out of the festival onto the long Regent Road now, walking toward town or trying to hail cabs. It's a good atmosphere, as it turns out, and we follow the swarm of bodies toward the pubs and bars. As for the short-circuit, the festival organisers are calling it a sabotage, an act of vandalism, but no one seems to really know what went on. After that, I haven't much of a recollection as it was half past midnight before we got off stage and I was pretty drunk by then. I kept drinking until the next day, apparently.

Bramley-Moore dock, Liverpool, 29/05/12

BEAUTIFUL THING/ STONE ROSES SUPPORT

It's a surreal experience, trundling beyond security gates into the Etihad stadium, seeing the roof of the enormous stage and the tiers of sky blue seats reaching up toward the sky like the frame of a huge empty cauldron. It can get the butterflies moving your gut, if you know what I mean.

I loved The Stone Roses as a teenager. I'd obsess over the lyrics to *Waterfall* and *Made Of Stone* and *Where Angels Play*. They were like old poems, I thought, full of Brigantine sails and twisted grills and holy shrines, but with a street-smartness too. A certain mystery lay at the core of the Roses, and like them or not, they cooked up some alchemy around that first record that few have been able to touch. For me, the strange shimmer of *Fools Gold* encompassed everything they were about. Like some skewed version of American desert noir, but for the north-west of England.

In a canteen in the bowels of the Etihad, I eat a good dinner. Better than I'd eat at home. As a rule, the bigger the gig, the better the catering is. On a table opposite, Public Enemy sit waiting for their food. Even in private moments they have that militancy about them. Dressed mostly in black, they talk quietly among themselves. Chuck D and Flavor Flav at opposite ends of the table, as if they're about to call some important meeting. I suspect they always come across like this. They're one of the greatest bands of all time if you ask me.

Anyway, there's no chance of me going over to say hello. No chance. I'm tongue-tied at the best of times, so I'm happy to observe them from a distance. Though one of our mates, Jay Redmo, thinks he's left his rucksack underneath their table. He walks over and starts rifling between where they're sat. I'm not sure Public Enemy understand a word he's saying. Either that or they think he's a cleaner. It's a brilliant scene.

We climb back to ground level and catch the end of the Buzzcocks. The stadium is brimming with people, even at this early point. The crowd are superb for us. There's usually a sense of detachment when I play gigs this size, but I feel every second of this one. I pick out a couple of people I know in the crowd, and suddenly I'm seeing this album cover in my head. I think it's Neil Young's *Time Fades Away*. I'm picturing that, for some reason.

Public Enemy nearly bring the stadium to its knees. The bass feels like the aftershock of an earthquake. We hear it from our dressing room directly behind the stage. We're well into drinking the rider by that point and by the time the Roses go on, we've inexplicably ended up at the other end of the stadium, watching bright red flares ghost into the night sky, the heave of people moving like a great sea.

One thing I noticed about the first Stone Roses reunion was that even in the huge venues they refuse to play like a stadium band. The delicacy is still there, the groove, the quiet moments. It takes a certain amount of guts to retain that, I think.

I'm watching people mill out of the stadium now. The huge floodlights have illuminated and everything is bright suddenly. I'm behind the stage again, drinking Guinness with Steve Diggle of the Buzzcocks, our dressing rooms next door to each other.

We get to talking and Steve tells me about the time in the mid-'90s when the Buzzcocks toured with Nirvana. He said that they'd been using these old televisions as stage props, and Steve would smash them at the end of every show. The way Steve told it, Kurt Cobain was interested in nicking the idea for Nirvana's set up. There was a moment in a soundcheck where Steve was teaching him the proper way to smash a TV without electrocuting himself. There's a knack to it, he said. Steve told me that Kurt never got to try it because the next week he'd shot himself, and they'd had to cancel everything and fly home. It was a sad time. I told him I was unaware they'd even played with Nirvana. Steve and I arrange to meet, maybe, when the Buzzcocks are in Liverpool next month.

We say our goodbyes and navigate our way down through the labyrinths of corridors and stairwells that lead to the outdoor car park. Soon we're in a fleet of black cabs, grinding down the M62 toward home.

In a strange way, the whole year seemed to coalesce to this point. Everything went off without a hitch, bar the over-eager door steward trying to bar me entry back *into* the stadium to watch Public Enemy. I didn't have the right wristbands, apparently. Apart from that, it was a flawless night. Too perfect for this diary, quite possibly.

Manchester, 17/06/16

DINAMO ZAGREB

When we lose our minds, it's a collective thing. We completely go. All of us, off the deep end. Synchronised. Something bottlenecks and then releases in some spectacular disgrace. A kind of freefall.

This is my first time in Eastern Europe. On my way through customs, I'm pulled aside by airport security. A stocky man in a white uniform asks me if I'm carrying any drugs. He goes through a long list of narcotics and I shake my head at each one before he stares blankly at me for a good twenty seconds. I almost expect him to ask *well, do you want any then?*

Zagreb is rainy and dull, which is in direct opposition to everything I've heard about Croatia. We're all in shorts and sunglasses and ready for a mooch around the bars and restaurants of the city. Still, navigating down the wide Zagreb streets with endless archipelagos of distant tower blocks glassing the sky is a good dose of sightseeing in itself.

After a night in the hotel drifting in and out of sleep, watching loops of dubbed Steven Seagal movies that seem to play on every channel, the next morning I feel ready to go.

We soundcheck early in the muddy, flooded field. The backstage area is sort of a partitioned gazebo with the names of the bands gaffered to each temporary room – Henry Rollins. Pennywise. Jake Bugg. Django Django. The Coral.

Our room has been stocked with a Croatian lager called Ožujsko. Crates of the stuff. There's nothing much else to do except sit around and drink it, until we go on to a small crowd that swells to a mob as the set builds.

Afterward, the backstage is full of artists. Some I recognise and some I don't. Jake Bugg keeps himself pretty isolated. He's had a hard time with the press recently and a part of me wants to say hello. I'm not sure why; I'm just aware how tough it must be fronting a thing on your own when you're as young as he is.

Pennywise are an American punk band who I know nothing about and suspect never will. Django Django I'm hoping to catch later – they play across the park from us, on the 'World Stage'. Outside, in the smoking area, Henry Rollins stomps around the temporary wooden boards that have been laid on top of the boggy ground. He looks serious.

I'm floating around the festival now. It's late and I think I catch part of Django Django's set. I'm not entirely sure if I'm honest – there are pint glasses of vodka orange in each of my hands and I've worked through one of them already. It's been a long day.

At the furthest reaches of the festival, I'm drawn toward something called the Tesla Tower; a hundred-foot-tall reproduction of Nikola Tesla's Wardenclyffe Tower, which was built and designed to transmit messages across the Atlantic using the earth's own electrical charge. It was never completed. This imitation transmits David Bowie songs from small speakers at its base. Kind of a double-homage with a link: Bowie played Tesla in the movie *The Prestige*. It stands enormous in the field like some kind of holy monolith, lit by shimmering emerald green lights that run along its skeleton frame.

I'm down at the bottom, splayed on a cluster of rocks, trying to light a cigarette. There's a point where I feel myself float slowly up to the top of the tower. Seriously. I'm hanging there in mid-air as *Let's Dance* plays from ground level.

I see the flood of people below me move like tiny ants. There's a feeling like I've got seven eyes, each one peering out from the bass drum of every band playing on each of the seven stages. As if I can see and hear everything at once. Some high electric current running across the bones of the earth and through me, into the ether. The song I can hear now is *Sound And Vision*.

Back in the dressing room, things have built to a fever. There's a chant going on and it's hard to know where it started or what it means. But everybody in our crew seems to have picked up on it: *Das, Gras, Pumpen-funf. Das, Gras, Pumpen-funf*, as if they're summoning some kind of demon. Everyone has that look in their eyes; the X-ray look that thinks it can penetrate walls, but can't see five centimetres past its own nose. The chant goes on. *Das, Gras, Pumpen-funf.*

We roll on like that for 45 minutes at least, the incantation gathering weight, the whole room shaking, and one of us falls clean through a wall, and I feel myself crying with laughter, wiping tears from the corners of my eyes with my sleeve.

Somewhere amid the melee, one of us offers Henry Rollins (who isn't happy about the noise) a blast on a joint, which apparently doesn't go down too well. Soon after, we're bundled into a van and driven back to the hotel.

I fall to sleep listening to a gang of Dinamo Zagreb fans singing in the street below the open window of the hotel room. It's a strangely comforting sound.

In the morning I wake up and realise everyone has left for the airport, everyone except for Alf from The Sundowners, who came along with us as a last minute guitar tech. He has a taxi waiting for us both. I probably only made the flight because of Alf.

When I arrive home I realise I've left most of my clothes, my deerstalker cap, comics, underwear and wallet at the hotel and I'll probably never see any of them again.

Zagreb, 20/06/16

T IN THE PARK CONVERSATION

"Yetts o'Muckhart. That's where we are. I've just seen a sign for it."

"It's like Crinkley Bottom around here."

"Have you seen it now? The Noel Edmonds theme park? All derelict and haunted."

"Haunted with the psychotic ghost of Mr Blobby."

"It's like Banksy's Dismaland, but darker."

"It is!"

"It gets used for illegal raves and stuff now y'know? The techno hippies have taken over."

"Remember when we were kids and we had that rave in John and Paul's house and banned Nathan from coming? But he came anyway and stood at the back of the room and over-raved, so he'd be accepted. Like, really putting everything into the dance. Remember?"

"Oh Jesus, that's devastating."

"And we put bin bags on the windows to black the room out like a nightclub."

"Bowls of Wotsits and Chipsticks."

"Ian and Paul pretending to skin up with banana skins like *The Prodigy Experience* album cover."

"We had the decks set up after we watched that Tupac film, *Juice.* But none of us could scratch."

"What happened to those decks?"

"We swapped them for a Megadrive."

"It was either Sega or Nintendo in those days. You couldn't be either. I was a SNES kid. All the way."

"Jay Pick was the first to have mixing decks though. In our area anyway. What an enigma."

"You always looked up to Jay Pick didn't you?"

"I put him on a pedestal, yeah. He used to do boxing training in his front yard with the skipping ropes and the bags and that."

"He went AWOL from the army later on, you know?"

"Which makes him cooler again."

"You always respected lads like him."

"I blame that movie *Stand By Me."*

Yetts o'Muckhart, 08/07/16

GOODBYE/ CORBRIDGE

It's weird. Sometimes the best nights are the ones when the pressure is off and you're left to your own devices.

In Corbridge, we go on stage relaxed, having wandered around the old town most of the day, satisfied in the knowledge that the night before, we'd delivered a good set at one of the big Scottish festivals, T In The Park.

The set we play tonight is loose and high-spirited. It reaches its apex when we hit the improvised section of *Goodbye*, the penultimate song in the set.

This is the point where things open up, you tend to deviate from what's been rehearsed and go wherever the mood takes you.

Tonight it becomes something like those early Pink Floyd UFO Club excursions, satellite blips and rolling oceans of echo beaming into the ether.

We lock into it, all of us collectively egging each other on, swinging between laughter and amphetamine intensity.

They stick with you, those kind of nights. You tend not to enter back into the earth's atmosphere until a couple of hours after coming off stage. It always seems to happen when we play *Goodbye*.

Once, during the recording of our debut album, we were upstairs in the communal room of Great Linford Manor, a residential studio somewhere in the middle of nowhere.

We were listening to the *Nuggets* garage compilation between playing pool, rolling joints and looking out for Rik Waller on TV, a stakeout that became known as *Waller-Watch.*

The idea for the song *Goodbye* appeared out of thin air suddenly, had us scribbling lyrics over the pool table on the back of a brown envelope. Most of the album was recorded by that point, but we all shot downstairs into the studio where the gear was still set up, waiting to be packed away.

We went at it non-stop and it was recorded later that night, all of it, the middle section and everything, just in time to make the album.

Corbridge, 09/07/16

BENICASSIM

Another terrorist incident in France tonight. A devastating attack which left more than seventy people dead. It's all over the news as I write this, between packing for tomorrow's trip to a Spanish festival called Benicassim. The media is in overdrive. I'll watch the rolling reports until the early hours, as Europe slips back into its petrified state.

The next evening we land in Barcelona, decamp outside the airport and wait for Big John to arrive in a hire car. After that, the two-and-a-half hour drive toward Valencia. We're splayed on the cool pavement, bodies and bags everywhere, a mass of scattered luggage and pale, exposed ankles.

Somehow, between trips back inside the airport to the bar and the toilet, two rucksacks are stolen from where we'd made the temporary base. Everybody swears they didn't see a thing. Amid the panic, it's decided they must have been nabbed by a skilled thief – there were no less than three people watching the bags at any one time – and the panic is exacerbated by the absence of any security in the building. Airport staff brush it off as if it were a daily occurrence, shooing us towards a non-existent staircase; *policia, policia.*

After a short stay in a motorway hotel, we're back on the road the next morning. I realise one of the bags that was stolen had my iPod in, which contained about ten years worth of songs. Rare stuff that I don't own any more. Still, what I lost doesn't compare with some of the others in the group; clothes. Prescription lenses. Medicine. Shoes. An expensive set of headphones.

Still, it's a warm day and spirits are high despite last night's theft. The landscape is unchanged from when I was here over ten years ago: distant, burned out hills that crumbling stone forts jut from. Olive groves running long past the horizon line. The chirp of crickets running through everything like some relentless electrical pulse.

The festival remains unchanged too, almost to the centimetre. The clinical bright white tarp of the dressing room area and the huge stage that looks out onto an arid field, framed by a brow of mountains that run off to the right, preserved exact in my memory.

At 1 o'clock, the heat is searing, relentless. We skulk off to a free bar that sits on a wide vista of multicoloured carpets and beanbags, shaded areas and sandpits. We sit and drink rum, while the day away listening to a Bowie cover band soundcheck. They go on for around two hours. They haven't quite got the nuances of Ziggy's operatic cockney, come off sounding more Dick Van Dyke than Thin White Duke. They keep slipping their own songs in too, which is bizarre.

I realise halfway through our own set just how many Muse fans are here. Every other person seems to have a T-shirt with their logo printed on the back. They're headlining this stage tonight, 45 minutes after we play.

Throughout the gig, our own fans are fantastic, and it's the newer, heavier songs that seem to unify everybody. I realise how schizophrenic our set must sound to people who don't know us so well. But that doesn't bother me too much; it's the way we've always listened to music. Mixtapes and playlists.

Back in the artist area, we're talking to Ian McCulloch. Echo And The Bunnymen have just come off stage and we're drinking around a circular upright table, a huge screen projecting the end of Muse's set into the backstage, lighting up the darkness with bright flashes of neon.

Meanwhile, McCulloch is in full comedic flow: he's written a tune about a dwarf and is explaining the hidden meanings behind the lyrics. We also (somehow) broach Mike Tyson's *The Undisputed Truth*, *The Sopranos*, Joe Fagin, existentialism and *Happy Death Men*.

He remembers a time when, "there were fucking 17 of you Coral-oids... you're easier to remember now there are only 12, you gang of gypsies." At some point, I offer to ghost-write Ian's biography and he says, "I'll fucking write it myself – I'm more than qualified." Which is probably true. The night rolls on, and he's got most of us creased with laughter. We'd stay if we could, but we've moved hotels from last night's – a glorified shanty where some of the toilets didn't flush. Our new one is much nicer, we're told, but two hours away, just outside Barcelona. And so we pile into the van and roll into the darkness, the van stereo turned up to breaking point as we sing our way back toward the city. There's a point where we pull over to piss, and a plague of winged bugs fills the van. They stay put, like demonic hitchhikers in migration.

Just behind us, the second van containing the crew and all of our instruments breaks down. From there, they embark on their own nightmare odyssey, which involves distress calls, broken petrol caps and attempts at bribing angry local policemen. They won't make it back until nine o'clock the next morning.

In the witching hour, we arrive in a plush, air-conditioned city hotel, and crawl off to our own rooms. I fall into bed, too drunk, too tired to enjoy it.

The next day in the departure lounge, the sharp jab of airport lager is like an elixir, all of us sat around a scuffed table in a place called Rib Shack, sunburned and parched as gringo explorers in the Sonoran desert.

Valencia, 16/07/16

IAN PLAYLIST/ DERBYSHIRE ROUTE

Baby Huey – *Hard Times*
BB King – *The Thrill Is Gone*
Freddy King – *Going Down*
Muddy Waters – *I Am The Blues*
Howlin' Wolf – *Spoonful*
Sir Joe Quarterman & Free Soul – *(I Got) So Much Trouble In My Mind*
Johnny Kidd & The Pirates – *Shakin' All Over*
Sly & The Family Stone – *Sing A Simple Song*
Wilson Pickett – *Engine Number 9*
Lee Dorsey – *Love Lots Of Lovin'*
Albert King – *Born Under A Bad Sign*

Motorway, 28/07/16

MOUNTAIN PEOPLE

Before the ascent, we'd come off the motorway somewhere near Stoke I think, but it was hard to tell through the fug of a three-day hangover. I'd been married only a few days earlier and the aftermath of the party was still etched into us all. It's decided there and then that the wedding celebration was a cross between *The Deer Hunter*, *Bridesmaids*, and Leland Palmer's exorcism dance in *Twin Peaks.* We all feel it today. The ache of hollow, tired bones.

At the last reaches of the motorway, we zoomed past an Amazon storage warehouse, which stood like some odd kind of cathedral, fortressed by high, barbed walls. I'd never seen one before. It must have been five football pitches long.

As we grunt through winding country lanes, a rolling mist descends slowing us to a crawl. Visibility is reduced to about twenty yards as we begin a nauseating climb toward the Peak District.

As ever though, the music is good. One of us came armed with a collection of dub and Lee Perry produced albums and a playlist of William Onyeabor's proto-space disco. The album of the day goes to the final Perry-produced album before burning down his legendary studio, the Black Ark. The album is called *Heart Of The Congos*. There is some murmured singing as we drive... '*Send my sons from afar and my daughters from the ends of the world...*' and for a time there, among the rolling mist and green hills, combined with the music, I almost imagined us scaling the Blue Mountains of Portland Jamaica, and then someone else remarks that, "we've been booked to play a fucking festival in the afterlife."

On arrival at the summit, we're cast straight back into England. The mist clears for an open, grey cirrus sky, and rain falling down in sheets. We're led to a row of corrugated containers, our holding pens for the day. There are gas heaters screwed to the wall, some beer, a bottle of rum and a bag of Walkers each. The smaller, multipack ones with about three crisps in. The seal is broken on the rum within minutes.

The sun comes out later, and we go out into the festival in search of food. Options include vans that go by the name of 'Pie Hard'. 'Rave Burger'. 'Wok And Roll'. I go for the pie and mash, and it does a good job in my gut and then everything seems brighter suddenly. The crowd is building toward the huge main stage where we're set to play, and there's a sense of something about to burst.

On my way back to the dressing room area, I spot a huge tent with a wooden cylinder loping out of the back. A sign says WALL OF DEATH: THE MOST THRILLING FAMILY ENTERTAINMENT IN THE WORLD.

Inside the thing, I'm looking down on a bright red and yellow painted floor, all sideshow bright and carnival, the smell of diesel and engine grease- working smells, and I see five or six motorcycles parked in a perfect circle, each one from a different pre-60s decade: Herald. Triumph. Norton. It's as if I've gone back to some depression-era medicine show. And then the Wall Of Death itself, enveloping the whole thing like some kind of solid oak bear pit.

Half an hour later there is the slam of a huge door. There are lads and dads here. People in biker leathers. Couples peering over the flimsy wire barrier. I feel the whole structure, the wood, the steel pins and metal roof beams move as I walk.

I can't hear the ringmaster's voice over the growl of motorbike engines. I just about hear him introduce himself as Luke Fox, before another rider, Klara goes spinning about the wall behind him, and everything begins to shake.

She's followed by another performer who's introduced, I think, as Ken Wolfe. He's in some sort of custom buggy contraption, and the three riders are weaving between each other, swooping up to the security wire and back down again. Everybody inside takes a step backward. There isn't even the slightest sign of any safety equipment. This is real entertainment. All the fun of the fair.

The gig isn't bad, either. The mist reappears as we play. A soft breeze too, which afterward, somebody said, "gave you all *the Stones at Altamont* quiffs."

Derbyshire, 28/07/16

BEAUTIFUL DAYS

Tents are crammed together in a field, hundreds and thousands of tents of different shapes and colours. They stare sadly through the grills of a wire metal fence as we enter the festival. They look like battery farm hens in the rain, muted and glum.

In a communal area behind a stage we meet up with John Leckie, who we worked with on the *Butterfly House* album. He's sitting at a picnic table and I ask him if he's been here long. He laughs and says he's "been here for three days and I have only washed my fucking hands once. I'm a mess."

You sit with Leckie and expect him to talk about being a tape-op for The Beatles, engineering Pink Floyd's *Meddle* album, or his long running dispute on whether he recorded the footsteps on their song *On The Run*. Instead, he'll sit and tell you a story about when he smoked Salvia in his living room and hallucinated he was four years old.

He's seen a lot in a half-century spanning career. He tells me about Syd Barrett's last session and how it completely fell apart, the sadness of it all. Also lately, he can't fathom "how to write my own fucking Wikipedia page."

When we were mixing *Butterfly House* in Liverpool, we'd go out with John at night and he'd love the bars that play old blues and soul, stuff that he considers his first love. He'd drink us under the table.

I wander out into the festival for some air, see how the crowd is. I stop at a record stall and start digging through a couple of crates. I uncover a seven-inch copy of *Johnny Remember Me*, the Joe Meek-produced track sung by John Leyton. It's a band favourite. We used to do a cover of it. That, along with The Teardrop Explodes' *Reward* and the old western song *Ghost Riders In The Sky*.

I jump on stage from the front, as I get lost on the way back. This festival was put on by The Levellers, and I'd wondered how we'd go down with a crowd of techno-hippie types in dreadlocks and fancy dress, but they turn out to be a great, receptive audience.

Afterwards, Leckie remembers the time he did a spoken word piece in the middle of one of our tracks. He read a bit from a *Hellblazer* comic, which was created by Alan Moore, who also wrote *Watchmen*.

"*The seaside was magic. Watching the tide dribble in mysteries of foam. Exploring weird alien worlds of tide pools and comics. Then, at night, the funfair."*

Later that day, we saw Alan Moore by chance, walking past the studio on Lark Lane in Liverpool. He came over and chatted for a while, signed our copies of *V For Vendetta* and *Hellblazer* that happened to be lying around.

Devon, 28/08/16

KING OF THE MAGIC SCREEN/ PORTSMOUTH JOURNEY

"If you think about it, he's the best of our generation."

"Who?"

"Spielberg."

"You think?"

"Yeah, it's like who did you listen to most growing up?"

"Floyd mostly. Pink Floyd."

"I bet you still listen to 'em."

"Oh, I always go back. I probably measure all bands against Floyd."

"That's what I'm talking about. Spielberg's the same. In fact, more so than Floyd because we were kids when he was peaking."

"What did he do?"

"I watched *E.T.* the other day and was crying my eyes out by the end."

"Ah yeah."

"*Duel*. Have you seen *Duel*?"

"Amazing. The way you never see the trucker. The evil might exist in the driver's mind. I love it."

"Well, think of that and then add *Jaws*. *Close Encounters*."

"Oh."

"*Poltergeist*."

"Oh yeah! *Carol Annnnn*. Jesus. What a movie."

"The first three *Indiana Jones*. The fourth doesn't count."

"You're right, yeah. Completely. *Gremlins*? He do that?"

"It's like for everyone in our generation, he kind of shaped our imaginations. With films, anyway. Know what I mean?"

"Did he do *The Goonies*?"

"He fucking *wrote* it.'

"Well there it is. Yeah. He's nailed it then. He's a Don."

"King of the magic screen."

Motorway, 27/08/16

VICTORIOUS

Driving into Portsmouth, you pass this huge floating crane that sits on a river outside a scrapyard for old ships. The thing is huge. Immediately you know you're in a tough town; even more so when you get nearer the shore, you see gangs of marauding kids heading toward the beachfront fair. I can't ever remember being here before, but it's growing on me already.

Bob Geldof is mooching around backstage in a frayed army jacket and fisherman's cap. He looks like he's dressed down for the occasion. He comes off looking like some kind of pantomime burglar. I think he's been out of the game for too long, cooped up on some country estate somewhere, where faded stars drink in ornate pubs and play football with each other on freshly mown private pitches.

In the dressing room next door, a new, hyped band from Australia called DMA's get ready to go on. It's strange, as they all wear stuff that I used to wear as a teenager around 1999. Baseball caps. Adidas Bluebird trackies with hot rock burns in the knee. Nike Air Max. I didn't expect that to creep back in fashion. I'm not sure it ever should. Just goes to show. They're alright lads though, and their set is a breath of fresh air in a sea of media trained bands.

While they're on stage, me, Ian and Duffy sit and talk around a circular table in the afternoon sun. I say to Duffy: "What was your first gig like?"

"I did the first two bars of The Beatles' *Day Tripper* and lost my bottle and walked off stage. He (pointing at Ian) was meant to sing vocals on it."

"Were you?" I ask.

"Me? Yeah. It was the school talent show. Was held in the lunch break. I turned up and there were loads of girls I knew there, and my arse went."

"What happened?"

"I just didn't get up when they called us."

"And I was left on my own with an acoustic, trying to sing *Day Tripper*, when I was only meant to be playing guitar on it."

"You threw him under the bus there!"

"Yeah. Even though I was meant to be singing, I sat there when he fucked it up, turning around to people and waving my hand in front of my nose. With absolutely no shame."

"Like that *Seinfeld* episode when Jerry…"

"Exactly."

"Technically that was the first Coral gig then?"

"Yeah."

"Yeah."

Later, as we leave, a huge Ferris wheel shoots synchronised illuminations toward the motorway, as if motioning us toward home. We decide to skip on the booked hotel and burst down the Tarmac to avoid the bank holiday traffic tomorrow.

By this point we've done a festival almost every week throughout the whole of summer. There's one left, near Birmingham next week, but I can feel a restlessness and boredom kick in. Everybody says they feel it. It's the end of the season and we're talking about writing new songs, like a scab that needs to be itched.

Portsmouth 27/08/16

FEAR AND LOATHING IN BRUM

We jack-knife straight through Birmingham. Right across its belly. It's four in the afternoon and we should have been at the festival site an hour ago.

From the motorway, we convulse through the city centre and continue for another couple of miles until the road narrows and becomes greener, studded with tall, weeping oak trees and you realise you're on something like a country estate, some anomaly of the city; a green oasis amid a sea of concrete. I never knew this place existed. There's a lake with black swans gliding across the water; trees shimmering with lights. It's more like something from *The Great Gatsby*.

After touching down backstage, we sit around a dining room table in a small tent. We're all feeling slightly seasick as the floor is on a gruesome slant. Scott Judge chips in, "Where the fuck are The Levellers when you need them?"

I'm staying in Birmingham on my own tonight. I've set up a DJ spot at a new club called The Night Owl, which specialises in northern soul, and the promoter has come to pick me up and take me to the club. We've come off stage and the dressing room is packed with people. It's our last festival of the year and everyone is making a night of it. Phil Etheridge from The Twang is here with his wife, and Paul and Greg from Skeleton Key band, The Cut Glass Kings.

The crowd dissipates eventually and Paul, Greg, me, and the promoter from The Night Owl jump a cab into town.

You know when a night takes on a kind of live-wire edge? It has that inexplicable feeling. Like the whole thing could turn on the strike of a match.

The DJ spot is a blur of lights and distortions, and while the club is great, I'm not sure what tunes I'm playing by the end of the set, around 2am. That's how these things usually go, you're pretty much on your own in a city you don't live in and you do what you have to do to survive, drink, take whatever to get you some Dutch courage.

We're in a club called Snobs next, on a high street somewhere. It's one of those places that has about four floors, a maze of roof terraces, rooms and staircases. It's impossible to get out of.

I'm in hat, jacket and boots with a military bag containing all my music and overnight stuff, a sweaty mess on the dance floor. The floor itself, everywhere, is seemingly covered in black ice and it's impossible to stay upright for more than five seconds at a time. I turn to Greg and say, "It's like an assault course in here," and he replies, "Worse. It's like *The Running Man*!"

After an hour I decide to make a break for it without saying my goodbyes as I'm yet to check into the hotel and it's near enough 4 o'clock.

I'm standing on the fourteenth floor of my hotel now, looking down on a huge roundabout that is hemmed in by a row of bright kebab houses.

I'm still pretty wired, so decide to head over there, have a smoke, maybe force something to eat. The lift seems to be stuck between floors so I take the stairs.

At the bright takeaway terrace, two beautiful fat black women are arguing with each other. One of them is halfway out of the door and wants the other to follow her outside for a straightener. Both of them are enormous.

"Seeka, come. Come outside Seeka. Come. Talk to me Seeka."

"My name's not even Seeka, it's Raelle."

"Come, Seeka."

"You don't even know my name."

"Come talk to me."

I duck into the adjacent kebab house to avoid what I think is about to happen. I order chicken doner and chips, for no real reason. I'm not even hungry.

The next thing that happens is a blur of bodies burst through the door like a wrecking ball. Bright colours and bracelets and hair beads. Huge arms flailing, throwing uppercuts and haymakers. The women are brawling. Ballsy, no-holds-barred street fighting. It's an amazing sight. I'm glued to it, as is everybody in here. Most of them have left their seats and are watching from the back wall. The women don't let up from one another. A whole table goes belly-up. They're covered in blood, both of them, before they both bundle back outside.

I turn around to see my meal in front of me. The man behind the counter is completely unfazed. He's laughing to himself. "Life's too short, my friend."

I nod and grab the polystyrene box of chips, dodge dark puddles of blood on the floor and make my way back over the roundabout to the hotel.

On my way up to the room, a man who looks exactly like Uri Geller sits on the stairs, picking at his bare left foot with a pair of tweezers.

Back on the double bed, I munch at the chips and doner meat, but the salt and chilli sauce are so potent that my heart is racing, as if I've necked some new synthetic drug, like Nuke from *Robocop II*. Eventually I nod off, but it's getting into the early hours.

I wake up to see the outline of two fellas standing at the end of my bed. They whisper at first.

"Churchy."

"Churchy, wake up."

"Churchy?"

"Is that Churchy?"

One of them pulls at the quilt and then shakes my feet. I open my eyes and spring forward as if waking from a nightmare.

"What the fuck!"

"Fuck, it's not Churchy."

They run out of the room, leaving the door slightly ajar, bright electric light from the corridor beaming onto the bed like a helicopter searchlight.

After locking the door behind them I sit up in bed for a time, wondering what just happened, all of it, the whole night.

And that's how the festival season ended.

Birmingham, 03/09/16

CHAPTER SIX

THE IN-BETWEEN

*Odd rehearsal. Finding Dion. Morning TV. Bird On A Wire.
The elusive John Carpenter. Dress Rehearsal Rag.
Horse Breaking. Malcolm Mooney's bacon butty.
When All The Birds Have Flown.*

ODD REHEARSAL

Duffy has been in touch via a group text to say, “Can we get in the room this week? I’m bored shitless.” So a rehearsal is arranged. During the day, three new songs appear: *Spirit Catcher*, *Runaway* and *Strangers In The Hollow*.

Foundations of a new album begin to emerge. Writing songs has never really been a problem for us, but feeling out the right textures and colours for an LP takes time. Still, getting three solid tunes under our belt feels good.

It goes the same way usually: James and Ian organising the backbeat in the way they do. Duffy picking out harmonies and passing notes. Me fiddling about on some old synth trying to find an interesting sound. Molloy feeling his way around ethereal, reverb drenched licks.

Later in the day a man from the council knocks on the door to complain about us dumping rubbish in the next door timber yard’s BIFFA bins.

Hoylake, 21/09/16

MOONEY

Malcom Mooney from Can came to our rehearsal room. Andy Votel brought him over from America for a string of UK shows. One of the gigs was Festival No. 6 in Portmeirion, where *The Prisoner* was filmed in the 60s. This was only a couple of weeks ago as I write.

The band that Votel put together was made up of Alf and Tim from The Sundowners and the young Murphy brothers, Phil and Danny, who’d played with virtually everyone who’d recently passed through town, including Mick Head and Johnny Echols of Love.

The sessions would take place in our rehearsal room. It was pretty exiting; the closest I’d got to Can was a brief backstage meeting with Holger Czukay after a gig in Cologne once. I couldn’t get a word out of him though.

Once, when we were just out of our teens, a few of my mates painted the name of one of Can's albums, *Ege Bamyasi*, in huge letters on the wall of Hoylake Co-Op. It stayed there for months. I think it baffled everyone in town but to us, it provided a secret source of power, some hieroglyphic energy that we fed off and laughed about for nearly a whole summer.

The way Alf tells it is that Mooney wanted to perform the *Monster Movie* album in full, and they were happy to learn it, being big fans of the band. On the first day in rehearsal, during a break, Alf returned with a bacon butty from a nearby café. It had Mooney obsessed. He couldn't work it out. "What is it? It's so dry!" He ended up signing the white Warburtons bread in black marker pen: MALCOLM MOONEY.

Mooney is an off-the-cuff improviser, and he ended up working the theme of the butty into the extended instrumental break of *Yoo Doo Right*. Apparently it had such an effect on him he had two microphones set up, and would launch into a volley of words, alternating between each one with lightning speed:

"Butty-butty-butty-butty-butty-butty-butty-butty-butty-butty-butty," his head moving from left to right in short, rapid salvos.

On the eve of the festival, I'm interested to know how the rehearsals have gone, so fire a text over to Alf. He texts back to say, "Yeah man, Mooney is boss, he's a sorcerer! He's totally unique. It's weird, sometimes you forget what's great about art and music and get down about it. Mooney reminded me that it's pure magic."

Hoylake, 22/09/16

DJ SET/ LIVERPOOL PSYCH FEST

Arzachel – *Queen St. Gang*
Neu! – *Negativland*
Hawkwind – *Opa-Loka*
Morgan Delt – *The System Of 1000 Lies*
The White Noise – *Love Without Sound*
Cat's Eyes – *Names On The Mountain*

The Myrrors – *Warpainting*
Faust – *So Far*
Stereolab – *I Was A Sunny Rainphase*
Skip Spence – *War In Peace*
Beak> – *The Meader*
Can – *All Gates Open*
Broadcast – *Pendulum*
David Axelrod – *The Death Of Juan Diaz*
Super Furry Animals – *Pan Ddaw'r Wawr*
Jane Weaver – *The Electric Mountain*
King Gizzard And The Lizard Wizard – *Mr Beat*
Focus Three – *10,000 Years Behind My Mind*

Camp And Furnace, Liverpool, 23/09/16

MORNING TV

The van pulls up outside the Camp And Furnace venue around 7 o'clock. I jump in after finishing up at Psych Fest. Despite not wanting to leave earlier, I'm ten minutes in the van and happy to be back travelling. The current argument is whether Aaron Neville has got a tear tattooed on his face, or if it's been mistaken for a huge mole. Turns out he has the mole and a tattoo, but the tattoo is a knife, not a tear. It takes almost an hour to reach this point.

At around one in the morning, we pull up to a hotel near Heathrow airport for a few hours sleep, the huge, floating hulks of Jumbo Jets ploughing through the night sky.

Early next morning we meet in the lobby and make the short journey toward the Sky TV buildings. I'm a bit disappointed by the complex, as it's basically a dull maze of concrete, almost like the opening sequence of *The Office* TV show. I was expecting something more like the OCP building from *Robocop*. Still, it takes us half an hour of messing around with security checks to actually get in the place, so the dystopian-future test checks out.

Inside, we do a soundcheck in a bright studio, a hyped-up floor manager in green glasses talking us through the rigours of live TV.

We perform a song and then step into a green room to wait to be interviewed. There is an imitation football pitch just outside, where Ian, Paul, Alf and Big John take penalties in front of TV cameras.

The interview is swift and painless. The host turns out to be a nice fella, sympathetic to our nervous interview patter.

After wrapping things up with a couple of band performances, we stand in a corridor waiting for Big John to give us the nod to leave. Ian is reading an article on his phone.

"My theory was true: Val Kilmer underwent therapy to help him break out of the Jim Morrison character."

"Really?"

"Yep. I called that one year ago. It's so obvious. After that *The Doors* movie, every role he plays is in the Jim Morrison character. In *Alexander* he *is* Jim Morrison. Seriously."

On the way home, a bottle of straight vodka gets passed around. Ian puts a compilation on, Rick James and Pat Benatar. 80s cocaine music. Songs that sound like the *Ghostbusters* theme.

You know you're home when you're on the motorway and see VOTE PIES painted in huge letters on a motorway overpass like an odd cryptic instruction. It really is an unofficial marker, a brilliant, surreal gateway back into the area I live in.

London, 24/09/16

THE WANDERER (James and Ian)

"So what happened the night you met Dion DiMucci?"

"We went down to London on the train, me and him (points). It was in a little jazz club. About the size of The Zanzibar."

"A little jazz club, yeah. Just Dion on stage with a guitar, on his own."

"And then he had a backing track for a couple of tunes. He'd reach over and press it and this this drum track would begin."

"Oh yeah, and he had these cockney doo wop fellas (laughs). These hired backing singers that would sing harmony every so often. But in a vague cockney accent that they couldn't conceal."

"I was stood next to Robert Plant. He was stood about how far you are from me now."

"Plant was there, Bobby Gillespie. Loads of people."

"And some woman who kept telling me off because I clapped dead loud next to her ear."

"So where did you meet him?"

"We jumped in one of those, what do you call them, rickshaw things."

"The fella driving it was playing the Paris Angels album, weirdly."

"And that's when we found Dion's hotel."

"How??"

"It was the guy who runs his label, Ace Records. I got his number off someone and just broke his balls. I was like, 'I wanna meet Dion.' He was like, 'Well, y'know, he might be tired,' and I was like, '*Where's the fucking hotel?*'"

"It was a fucking mission. It was about an hour away. And then he was just sitting there wasn't he? In a bar, on his own."

"There were a few record people milling about, but that was it."

"People would go over and sit down one at a time and talk to him. So I was like to him (points), 'There's Dion, I'm going over. End of. And he was like, 'Don't, don't!' But Dion was sound with it. He just looked at me and said 'Yo!' and shook my hand. I told him I was a massive fan and gave him a few of our albums. Then I started asking him about his tunes..."

"He spoke about The Everly Brothers mostly."

"And then he (points) came over and took over the conversation."

"Dion's just a force of nature, like."

"Among people who properly know the history of rock'n'roll, he's a giant."

"You just have to look at the people who inducted him into The Rock And Roll Hall Of Fame. Lou Reed. Paul Simon. Billy Joel. D'you know what I mean? Like fucking masters of song writing aren't they? Dylan loved him. His book is great you know? I found it again the other day. It goes into the history of The Bronx before it was decimated. All the Italians in the tenements. He tells it brilliantly."

"That's where *Roots And Echoes* comes from. It's the name of the opening chapter."

"That guy was there as well, the one who wrote *The Drifter*. Northern soul classic."

"Harsh when Dion was telling us about that *No One's Waiting or Me* tune."

“About the girl committing suicide in the hotel?”
“Yeah, you could see he was still hurting about that.”
“Well, he’s a soulful guy, isn’t he?”

Rehearsal room, 12/10/16

HORSE BREAKING

Mysterious ninth planet may have caused the solar system to tilt – The Guardian.

Rehearsal day. New songs in the set for the December tour. *Arabian Sand*, *I Remember When*, *Bill McCai*, *Shadows Fall*. Jim from The Sundowners is drafted in to play percussion parts. We start with *Arabian Sand* and go at it frenetically until it feels easier to steer. Songs like that can run away with you if you’re not careful. It’s almost like breaking a wild horse. Not that I’ve ever done that.

Later in the day Jim rings to say that he’s been offered a steady tour playing drums for Ian Broudie throughout the whole of December. He’d be stupid to turn it down. We sit around for a while deciding whether to replace him and somebody says that Jack Prince, who plays drums for Bill Ryder-Jones, might be a good shout, but we’d have to square it with Bill first.

20/10/16

THE FOG

I ride the early train to town. I’m picking up some electrical supplies for the tour. Plugs, leads, adaptors. Plus, my phone’s broken so I go into the Apple store in Liverpool One and drop it off before making an escape.

While I’m waiting on the repair, I head up to The Liverpool pub near the Albert Dock. I bump into James and Ian outside. They’re on their way home. James has been in Parr Street studio mixing a new band called Cabbage. He and Blossoms scored a recent Number One chart album with Blossoms debut, and he’s been producing bands steadily since then. Ian's been mixing Serpent Power's latest album, the group he formed with Molloy. It's almost done, he says, and sounds like an incestuous affair between Aphrodite's Child, Captain Beefheart and ABBA. They hail a cab and jump in it and I say I might see them later.

Duffy texts to say that John Carpenter is playing in town tonight and I should try and blag a ticket from somewhere. He's going with his brother, John. I'd forgotten all about this, so I jump in a taxi to the Olympia venue to see if I can get a ticket from a tout. There's nobody outside when I pull up, so I walk around the building a couple of times. From inside, I can hear the piano melody from the *Halloween* soundtrack. He must be soundchecking. I'm sick that I'll miss this. Defeated, I start the walk back into town, still humming the melody, playing an irritated kind of air piano as I trudge toward the underground.

28/10/16

BIRD ON A WIRE

Donald Trump is elected president of
the United States of America.

I wake early, around 6.30am, and can't get back to sleep. I head downstairs to check the results of the US election. I switch on the TV and Donald Trump is standing on a podium giving a victory speech. I hadn't seen that coming. It's like an interview from the WWE wrestling bouts we used to watch in John and Paul Duffy's loft.

A couple of days later we rehearse the new set. It's under a month until the tour now and things are beginning to take shape. The set is bulked up with a few more singles this time around, and seems pretty infallible.

I make the familiar walk to the practice room with Duffy and Jack Prince, who's playing some percussion on the tour.

We trudge up the stairs and hear the band playing a hypnotic song I haven't heard before.

It still amazes me how easily the band can conjure up a tune. You'll walk up the stairs maybe 15 minutes late for rehearsal and hear a new song nearly all the way complete. It can happen that way. Other times we have to grind an idea out and it'll have to be killed and resurrected a couple of times before it emerges in the right skin. Sometimes you have to trick them into existence before they start dictating how they think they should sound.

In the mid-set tea break, there's a conversation happening on the couches next to the huge, broken flat-screen TV we received from Sony once, in receipt of a gig.

"Remember the fella who worked in The Beatles shop in town?"

"Yeah. Mike Lennartney?"

"Yeah! Did he actually change his name to Lennartney or did you blag that?"

"I actually don't know any more."

"Well, listen to this: John knows a girl who worked with Matt Groening and she says he based the character 'Comic Book Guy' from *The Simpsons* on him."

"Fuck off."

"Honestly."

"I fucking knew it."

10/11/16

SHOT/ THREE-WAY CONVERSATION

"Have you got any funny memories of those Oasis tours?"

"Probably, yeah."

"I dunno why, but my memory's shot from that period. And it'd be good for the book."

"What about when we got bladdered with Liam in Berlin and he got us on his bus and made us eat sushi for the first time in our lives?"

"Oh yeah, that's decent."

"Or when we played *The Curse Of Love* in soundcheck and Noel thought I was singing '*all the birds have flown*' in the chorus, so I went and wrote that song anyway."

"I didn't even know about that?"

"Liam getting stoned in Madrid and telling us he used to listen to Simon And Garfunkel records at half speed, and that's what he thought we sounded like."

"Or that!"

"Or when we listened to their album demos in the studio and got them to re-record *Soldier On*, which they'd forgotten about."

"I remember that. I love that tune."

"Or the fact that when we came to record *Roots And Echoes*, they agreed to let us use their studio for free. But it turned out to be our most expensive album by a long stretch, because the hospitality, the food and booze, was so good that we ended up staying two weeks longer than we should have."

"It was like a holiday wasn't it?"

Rehearsal room, 11/11/16

DRESS REHEARSAL RAG

Final rehearsals begin. Old songs appear in the set. Heavyweights that we'd held back earlier in the year in favour of new album tracks. Songs like *Bill McCai* and *I Remember When*. It feels like a bulletproof run.

We rehearse one of the new ideas, *Strangers In The Hollow*, and it comes together pretty quickly. James strums it out and sings the verse, while Ian plays one of those click-clack rhythms you might hear from the fairground Waltzers. Duffy follows the melody with the bass.

I use the Philicorda organ with a slap-back delay pedal and it begins to reflect itself, chugging in that Chess Records way, the haunted way. We finish rehearsals on a high.

I jump in the car after that. I'm not sure where I'm going, but I'm driving through dark streets listening to *Veedon Fleece*, council workers in high-vis jackets putting up Christmas trees and bright decorations all over town.

17/11/16

LIVE SET

Chasing The Tail Of A Dream
White Bird
Simon Diamond
I Remember When
Jacqueline
Pass It On
In The Morning
Calendars And Clocks
Holy Revelation
She's Got A Reason
Don't Think You're The First
Miss Fortune
Million Eyes
1000 Years
Bill McCai
Shadows Fall
Arabian Sand
Fear Machine

Goodbye
Dreaming Of You

CHAPTER SEVEN

MEMORY TAPES (II)

Breaking into Motown. David Letterman. First time in Japan.
The holy mountain. Bodysnatchers.
Lost in Almeria. A band of gypsies.
Twenty-four hour cityscapes.
The music box hotel.

AMERICAN DREAMS

America again, and zooming through border towns; hot days in Amarillo and Denver, the outskirts of Detroit in one-room hotels, and then the city itself; walking up a crowded highway toward the Motown studio and taking the guided tour.

Inside the Motown building we were led around while a tour guide reeled off facts that we already knew. At some point we slipped away from the group and tiptoed back toward the locked studio. There, we ghosted through a partition in the wall and entered the recording space; a drum kit in the corner, a broken piano at a painted wall. A vintage microphone on a polished stand. *My Girl*. Smokey. James Jamerson. You could feel them.

At a truck stop in Arizona we bedded down in a novelty hotel built in the style of some deep-south bordello from the 1800s. White painted carriage wheels and fake chandeliers hanging from ceilings and walls. In a burlesque restaurant on the same retail park we sat and ate steaks the size of our arms. The restaurant was built in the style of an old speakeasy. There was a stage beyond the seating area where an extended playground swing hung down from the high rafters.

At some point, a young burlesque dancer mounted the swing and began moving, swooping back and forth like a pendulum, kicking her legs going forward and bringing them in going back. The swing must have gone fifty-foot high into the ceiling. We were transfixed. When she reached the top, she kicked this huge bell that rang out all around the restaurant.

After the show she walked around the tables introducing herself as Evelyn-Rose. I stared back, slack-jawed. I'll never forget it.

Days later, a show in Seattle had to be cancelled when we were snowed in at a truck stop south-east of there, near Denver. We didn't do anything much but lurk around a gas station, smoke weed and watch movies.

We camped out with Supergrass (who we were touring with) on the adjacent bus sometimes, singing with an old lap-steel that Mickey, the bass player, had procured from a thrift store. They boarded a plane to make that night's gig.

When we ran out of weed, our road crew ventured out into the nearby bars to test the water. They were a tight crew who'd come up in the 80s with The Stairs and The La's and Marshmallow Overcoat, and they weren't phased by anything really, and I saw them on the last night on my way back from the all night garage, bags of crisps stuffed under my arms.

They were in the corner of the car park sharing a joint with a couple of local truck drivers. They gave me the thumbs-up as I skulked past them toward the bus and a coffin-bunk, to lose myself for three days in a curvature of quilts and dream about California while the snow thawed.

LETTERMAN

On our first day in America, we were booked in to play the *Late Show With David Letterman*, the nightly talk show that broadcast live out of Manhattan.

There was us, Alan Wills, Joe Fearon, and a couple of English music journalists. We were all ushered to the top floor of this Trump Towers style building by flat headed Italian-American security guards who'd say things like "Hey kid, get your mitts off that vase," in a way I'd always imagined them to.

On our way into the studio, we passed a sprawling wardrobe department. There was a rack of shirts out in the corridor, to whom a passing employee told me belonged to the recently wound-up *Seinfeld* show. Without thinking, I pulled my sweatshirt over my head and took something from the rack and buttoned it up.

We played *Dreaming Of You*, and afterwards Letterman jumped up, shook each of our hands and made a little small talk. That's me in Kramer's silk shirt. You can see it. Clear as day. Reflecting the studio lights back like a mirrorball.

THE HOLY MOUNTAIN

All we'd heard was that the Fuji Rock festival was held somewhere near the peak of the huge Japanese mountain of the same name. That turned out to be untrue, though it was somewhere in that region, and we travelled up in a long, single decker bus that grunted up the winding roads.

Before setting off, we'd visited these beautiful ornate Buddhist temples, sampled Korean barbecues and street-corner food shacks, drank in low-lit Izakyas and sat up in tall hotels, wracked with jetlag, watching game shows that gave you square eyes.

And you'd walk down the road and be so tall that people would stare, and you'd feel like Bill Murray or somebody, some past it film star stopping over the weekend to film a whiskey commercial.

We'd spend full days and nights ducking in and out of vintage toy shops to buy movie figurines that were impossible to find in England. I still have an original Lo-Pan model from the movie *Big Trouble In Little China* that sits on my front windowsill.

On a neon-lit street, I saw a teddy-picker machine, only instead of cuddly toys at the bottom, it had huge live blue lobsters stacked on top of each other in brown murky seawater. This was outside one of many arcades where there'd be long, snaking queues of people waiting to play Pachinko, sort of a Japanese Pinball game, only without the flippers. The locals were obsessed.

At the festival, minutes before going on stage, we bumped into Bruce Johnston from The Beach Boys. He was sitting on the step of a mobile drinking a coffee, wearing his standard-issue Hawaiian shirt and shorts. He was great, too, genuinely affable and open.

"Keep your publishing," he kept repeating to us as he talked. "Whatever you do man, don't let them tear out your soul."

BODYSNATCHERS

Because of our aversion to travelling in the early days, we dreamed up a concept that might solve the problem. For the long-haul excursions, anyway.

It was thought that we could hire and train a band of Japanese impersonators, lookalikes that would tour exclusively through the Far East, moonlighting as us. They'd be an impression of the band, almost as if we'd been taken over by bodysnatchers. We thought the concept was ahead of its time, and that it would save the record company thousands in travel fees. We pitched the idea to them, but inexplicably, they laughed it off.

LOUIE THE FLUTE

It was Jase Melia who suggested him. We were after a flautist to play over the newly recorded *Don't Think You're The First* single.

Louie arrived stoned, and shot through his parts in a couple of takes at most, adding some great lines of his own. Louie was small with a tight, knotted mop of hair that covered his eyes and when he played the flute it was all you could see of him. He used to roll big joints that looked like cigars, with no tobacco in.

We filmed the video for that single in a woodland not far from the rehearsal room. We rented a van for the day, a huge mob of us, and spent most of the time wandering the thick bracken, climbing trees and miming along to the track.

Louie was generating his own myth that day. He wore a scarf around his neck and a trilby that gave him the appearance of some kind of time traveller from a Jules Verne novel. He was sipping from a huge flask, which, as he explained, was full of 'steaming mushroom broth'. I watched him and tracked his passage as he lapsed slowly into an alternative dimension.

When the filming was wrapped and it was time to leave, we made our way through the muddy terrain and back to the van. As we were about to get in, Louie was stood on a high sandstone outcrop that we'd parked in the shadow of.

"I'm gonna make my own way home lads, don't worry about me," Louie announced.

And with that, he disappeared back into the dense forest. I can say, hand on heart, that I haven't seen or heard from Louie the Flute since.

1000 YEARS VIDEO

Almeria, they said. Southern Spain, where a lot of the old westerns were filmed. *A Fistful Of Dollars*. *The Good, The Bad And The Ugly*. *Johnny Yuma*. Even parts of *Lawrence Of Arabia*. The list is endless. Shoot the video there, they said. It looks like Arizona you see; all sandstone bluffs and tumbleweeds. There's even the remnant of a studio set somewhere, way out on the scorched flats. A movie ghost town.

The record company told us that they'd rented a villa for us to stay in. But we won't pay for your flights, they said, or the transit of any props. You'll have to take those yourselves, as hand luggage. And make the video exciting, they said. Nothing too mind-bending.

To us, the landscape looked extra-terrestrial. Almost like Mars. Thinking of themes for the video, the first idea was of an astronaut lost in a Sergio Leone desertscape. It wouldn't be easy with the budget, but we had a great director on our side, James Slater, who we'd collaborated with before.

So a spacesuit was called for. A horse and rider, a gas mask, a dead octopus, a flamenco dancer, and an Elizabethan wig. The plan was to weave some thread of a storyline using those elements. It turned out to be the last video budget we'd ever receive.

I found it hard to breathe in the space helmet. It was late summer over there, and we were filming all day in the searing heat. I'd do one or two runs of taking an invisible bullet through the chest, or exploring cliff high faces and dried out river beds, before resting for half an hour to cool down.

Before the last day of filming, the director had asked me to get up early, before sunrise, to capture the final shot of the video in which the astronaut goes on a hallucinatory journey that winds up on a beach. It's here he realises he is marooned on the alien planet and can't get home.

The Spanish camera crew picked me up at 4am. in a camper van. We trundled down roads of dilapidated pink painted villas, and dirt tracks that cut through fields full of circular hay bales. Everywhere was silver-grey. I was too tired to find conversation with the crew, so I just stared at the scenery.

It was easier to film in the cool dawn. The beach was perfect; golden sand and a clear azure blue sea. There was a shaded wood just beyond the sand and rock pools and gullies in hidden enclaves.

After the final shot, I took a short walk down the beach before the rest of the band arrived. I was still in full costume.

On my way back, I spotted the camera crew packing their gear away. There was a solitary sun lounger which had a towel draped over it emblazoned with the American flag. I put the space helmet on and sat there for a while in character, imagining what it would be like to be stranded on a distant satellite somewhere in the far reaches of the universe.

And then the camera crew, lads and girls, stripped naked suddenly and jumped in the sea. I watched them from my perch in full spacesuit, trying to lift the helmet visor up with my padded gloves so I could light a cigarette, a new sun rising softly over the distant water.

THE JONATHAN ROSS SHOW

It's a strange feeling being sat in a BBC television studio with Jim Carrey and Johnny Vegas, and you still live in your parent's house. Chris Tarrant was there, trying desperately to look important among the weight of personality. He was ignored, came across like a cringe-worthy Steve Coogan character, Gareth Cheeseman or Saxondale, but with less charisma. Our attention was fixed to Vegas mostly, who's underground film *Who's Ready For Ice Cream?* was played constantly on our tour bus around that time.

We were invited to perform *Pass It On* and had spent the day going through a set of camera rehearsals. The premise of the show was to sit in a sort of backstage green room while guests are summoned out to be interviewed. While we weren't actually getting interviewed ourselves, part of the show involves a cut to the green room to catch the guests' reactions to the patter on the studio floor.

Jim Carrey sweated through the whole thing. His assistant kept making panicked shuttle runs to and from his dressing room to bring fresh towels to dab his wringing wet face with. He went through about three shirts. And Johnny Vegas, half cut, in full flow, regaling the room with tales of Timotei shampoo, St Helens Glass and *Northwest Tonight* presenter Gordon Burns, oblivious to everyone except him and us. It went like that for two hours or so; us doubled up in stitches on the couch. Tarrant getting progressively more annoyed. Carrey remained in the corner, half-listening in, as if we were speaking in some lost Venusian dialect.

CHRISTIANA AND THE MUSIC BOX HOTEL

Midway through our first tour of Europe, most of us still in our teens, we took a detour and stopped off at Christiana, an army barrack turned hippie retreat that lies in the east of Copenhagen. It was taken over in 1971 by a group of anarchists, who declared independence from the country of Denmark.

As part of the takeover, new laws were written up, separate from the Danish constitution, ones that made the sale of soft drugs legal, so long as they happened within the confines of the barracks.

In the last decade those laws have been quashed, but around 2002, they were wholly in effect. I think it was about the second time we'd been there. And that day in Christiana, I ate a flattened Mexican magic mushroom the size of a hubcap. It was Halloween.

There were three of us, I think, who'd chosen to embark on that particular odyssey, and soon we were wandering around the antiquated city like apparitions, wide-eyed and uneasy, sometimes crippled with heaves of laughter. Carved pumpkins in the doorways of restaurants sprang up like cartoon horrors, glowing in the dark. Bizarrely, we bundled into a steak house and ordered enormous racks of ribs that looked like human corpses.

By midnight, the hotel we were staying in felt like some kind of giant music box. In my white and sky-blue painted room, I began feeling like I'd been shrunken down into a miniature of myself. I thought the only course of escape was through water, so I ran a bath and waited for it to fill while I watched from the tile floor.

Once in, I could hear the others laughing through the next-door wall. Someone had flicked the TV channel to an X-rated movie featuring an actor who was "the spitting image of Doctor Karl Kennedy from *Neighbours*." I stayed in the bath for four hours.

After returning home from that European tour, aged 21, I'd dropped a stone in weight and resembled one of, as my dad said, "Ray Harryhausen's skeleton army in a Kickers jumper."

My mum thought I was on heroin, and so I explained that most of our touring budget went on McDonald's breakfasts, Haribo, Roysters crisps and CD Walkman batteries, but it mostly went on bags of skunk that travelled clandestine in the trailer, strapped to the inner rim of some tom-tom case or valve amp. Food was never much of a priority.

The weight loss, I explained, was a combination of all of these things, but also due to tour managers who believed "you play better when you're hungry."

THINK TANK

On tour with Blur, a cruel European winter that burrowed down deep into your bones, turned the huge arenas we were playing in into temporary ice rinks. Our second album had not long been out, and the record company were eager for us to go and conquer the continent, especially the main Sony territories like France and Germany.

We met Damon Albarn in Blur's dressing room while he was eating pieces of raw ginger, to "toughen his throat up". He was in the middle of recording a solo album at the time called *Democrazy*, and you'd see him hunched over a primitive tape machine in some unmarked room in the catacombs of whatever venue we were playing.

There was a lot of waiting around on that tour, as we'd bought onto

Blur's catering, so there wasn't the daily venture into the unknown to find food.

I remember James playing *In The Morning* in the cafeteria one day, sat on one of the canteen tables with an acoustic. It was an idea around then, a throwaway nursery rhyme that he thought was a laugh, something we'd try possibly if we had time in the studio. It went on to be the most played radio single the next year, beating Beyoncé's *Crazy in Love*. I think a lot of great singles are made that way. You hear about them coming to the writer like a bolt from the blue. As if they were a conduit somehow for some feeling in the ether.

We were playing once in Cologne I think, when Holger Czukay from Can showed after a gig, and he was like some enlightened Buddha, laughing at everything like he was on some other plane.

I wanted to speak to him, ask him about the old cinema they'd lived and recorded in around the *Ege Bamyasi* album, the German B-movies they'd recorded the soundtracks for. But someone had given him an early version of the iPod, and there was no way of breaking his curiosity. He was engrossed.

Somewhere on that tour, we filmed the video for *Bill McCai*. It was Holland I think, Amsterdam. The first couple of times we'd been had been real eye-openers. We'd wander the canals and red-light districts, through three-story brothels, gawping in such disbelief that we drew laughs from some of the hookers. One night a man on a bridge got stabbed, right in front of our eyes.

By the time of the Blur tour, we were different. More road-hardened, spotty freaks in bug-shades and trapper hats, living out of buses and bags, fine-tuned to the rules of the streets and seedy 24-hour cityscapes.

CHAPTER EIGHT

HOME RUN

An art exhibition. UFOs on the motorway. The sound of silence.
The long and winding road. The end. The future.
Trapped in Glasgow. Three dreams.
Mystery house. Geoff Barrow.

EXHIBIT

It starts at the rehearsal room, as it always does. It's an unusually warm day for this time of year, and I'm sweating in a huge sheepskin coat. Travelling companions today include Big John, Carl, James, Ian, Duffy and Molloy. Jack Prince, who's been roped in to play percussion will jump on board tomorrow for the first show in Leeds.

A conversation on the way plays out like this:

"Remember when we were young, and Connor held that shop up with a gun and then knocked at your house?"

"Shocking. Yeah, and he asked me to stash this sports bag for him."

"We were staring at it in your bedroom going, '*Shall we open it?*'"

"Yeah and we did, and all that was in there was a pack of custard creams and a pair of undies."

"Yeah. Like, why did he stash it then?"

"We'll never know."

We listen to a great lost Dion And The Belmonts album from the 70s, recorded after some of the Belmonts returned from the Vietnam war.

"What about when Jan Molby came to our school, and played against everybody on the footy pitch. Like, the whole school versus Jan Molby."

"And we still couldn't get the ball off him."

"He used to drink in dad's pub in Moreton, playing darts in his footy boots with a pint of Guinness, straight from training."

"Some player."

The tour starts at the RedHouse art gallery in Harrogate, of all places. There is to be an exhibition of the artwork Ian has created with his girlfriend, Anna Benson that makes up the sleeve of the new album. There are framed screen prints hanging in the studio space, a huge brass Victorian diving helmet that was used in our recent photo shoots, and a space dedicated to the in-sleeve lyrics that I typed out on an old typewriter. The whole thing is presented superbly, and the general feeling from people is that we probably should have done this a long time ago.

We've always fought to keep our artwork in-house, mostly through Ian, Anna and my older brother, Kev, who shot a lot of our early photographs. You get a better sense of what the band are about that way.

To round the night off, James and Molloy play an acoustic set to a packed room, including a great version of Bob Marley's *How Many Times*. The place is so busy that I can't even see the stage so I stand in a doorway at the back listening in.

On the short drive home, Keggo texts to say:

"Company leader to Raven, come in Johnny, identify Baker Team! Rambo, Messner, Ortega, Coletta, Jorgensen, Berry, Krakauer, confirm Johnny?!..."

Harrogate, 07/12/16

CATHEDRAL

On the way to Leeds, breaking reds to beat the rush hour traffic. We've left too late today, as it was the early hours when we got home from the exhibition in Harrogate. As soon as we hit the motorway, we start talking about production for the next album:

"I've been recording a lot of guitars just going straight into the desk lately, and using the distortion from there. There's no amplifier spill. Sounds unbelievable."

"We should try that for the new album."

"Like all that weird Lindsey Buckingham solo stuff we were listening to before. It's like that. Or Geoff Emerick, know what I mean? Really dry and present."

"If we're gonna go for it on this album then we might as well just do it and not hold back. There are some good singles already."

"Yeah, I feel like we did *Distance Inbetween* and the record label let us do what we wanted and backed it. So we should go for something a bit more song-based now, change it up a bit. Like some kind of surf thing. The Beach Boys in Llandudno."

"I'm completely into that side of us as much as the weird side, to be honest."

"It's almost like the opposite of the last album."

"We'd be repeating ourselves otherwise, wouldn't we?"

It's been dark from about 2pm. onwards today. We ghost into Leeds and pull up at the new Academy venue, which is a huge, beautifully converted cathedral. Soundcheck isn't for another hour, so we go for a wander down to the Christmas markets, where there are the usual temporary log-cabins, mulled wine stalls and nativity scenes stood awkwardly in outdoor car parks. "It's just like Bethlehem," somebody says sarcastically. "More like Brex-lehem," someone adds.

We go on almost an hour later than advertised. The gig is belting; a hothouse of energy, and is rammed to the back doors. We burst through it, pack up and leave swiftly for the journey to Glasgow.

After what seems like an age of trundling down slow motorways, we reach the Travelodge. I collapse in bed watching a documentary on the American/ Russian space race in the 1960s.

I fall to sleep watching footage of a monkey in a NASA shuttle being blasted into the stratosphere, thinking I'd felt like that once or twice, trying to sleep at the end of a Skeleton Key club night.

Leeds, 08/12/16

GLASGOW RETURN LEG

Before the journey to Glasgow, we eat a full English breakfast each, sat around a long table in a Little Chef cafe. We're talking about the *2000 A.D.* comic series; how it can be hard sometimes to get a grip on the back stories of the characters because it's been going for so long.

James says, "When I was younger my dad made me work on this hog roast van, and the fellas who owned it would have stacks of *Judge Dredd* in the back. That's how I got into it."

After we've eaten, I take a photograph of the grey motorway and the reflection of the ceiling lights in the window makes it look as if there are two perfect jellybean shaped UFOs hovering overhead. I can't stop staring at it. I think about selling it to one of those pulp newspapers that run headlines like *Hillary Clinton Gives Birth To*

Inter-dimensional Otter.

As the van heaves up the dark motorway we listen to an early mix of The Sundowners new album, then an Abyssinians compilation.

I'm sitting on the middle row of seats between James and Ian. We start throwing around some ideas:

"I was thinking something like *Closer To The Heart Of Time* might be a good title for the next album."

"I like it, yeah. It's quite psychedelic isn't it?"

"It's off that John Cheever story I was telling you about."

"I only know *The Swimmer* by him."

"I forget the name of it now. I'll lend you it, you'd love it. Anyway, if that doesn't work we could go for something more direct."

Ian says, "I've got a good idea for some artwork here. I did it the other day." He takes out his phone and shows us a photograph of a collage he's put together.

"That's great. It's a bit like those animations from the 1930s."

"Yeah, crossed with *El Topo* or something. Or a Mexican cartoon."

Eventually, we pull into the city.

I walk into the huge venue that lies in the middle of the Gorbals area of Glasgow, on Eglington Street. Last time I was here I was mistaken by a group of girls for Dean Gaffney. It was a crushing moment, and one I'll never forget.

After the show, a lad who's travelled all the way from Brazil is ushered into the dressing room by Big John. He introduces himself as 'Wanderson'. He's half-hyperventilating as he speaks, so somebody passes him a Guinness to calm his nerves. He sips it and makes a face like he's drinking coal tar, so I pass him a Corona. He says he's from a town in the north of Brazil near Sao Paulo, and has flown over just to see us. It's a touching thing to hear, somebody travelling over five thousand miles to see one of your shows.

Following that, I DJ an aftershow party with Keggo standing next to me on stage. We play air saxophone to Beck's *The New Pollution* and somebody takes a great photo, both of us in silhouette like the old jazz kings, though this is two English lads in a strange Glasgow boozer, not really knowing where they are or how they are going to make it back to where they're staying.

Glasgow, 09/12/16

VICTORY LAP

Outside a pub called The Snaffle Bit in the west end of Glasgow, we find ourselves trapped in the van while a three-mile long Orange Lodge march passes by. The thing is huge, and constitutes thousands of people. I watch it from a backseat window, reading some of the embroidered banners that are on show:

Castle Perth Proddy Boys
Murray Club Partick Branch
Young Calvary Flute Band
Young Calvary Volunteers
Lest We Forget
Larkhall Purple Heroes
Black Ridge Thistle
The Brave Thirteen

The procession passes after about 45 minutes. We've attracted some puzzled looks from the participants, not least a fella with a scar from his ear to the corner of his mouth who pressed his nose up to the window as if to say *move the fucking van*. Women in wartime nurses uniforms and old folks on mobility scooters bring up the rear.

On the drowsy journey toward Liverpool, I see:
Two cows lying down on the hard shoulder of the motorway.
A microlight pilot hurtling toward a dense cluster of trees.
An aeroplane frozen in mid-air.
A car-barn in a field with VOTE LEAVE painted on it in huge white letters.
A family sitting on an embankment near their broken down car.
A child wandering down the slope toward the road.

Off the motorway near Carlisle, we pull into a service station called Tebay, which any touring band will tell you is the Mecca of service stations, the holiest of holy lands. We sit down and eat huge roast dinners, all of us.

James tells me over lunch: "I had a dream within a dream within a dream last night. I'm not sure if I'm actually out of it yet."

"What happened?"

"It was like a really stupid version of that movie *Inception*. It's baffled me."

"Go on."

"So it starts with me getting driven to Bidston train station, I don't know who by, and She Drew The Gun are there, but like, *Tank Girl* versions of the band, with green hair and stuff. And they've got loads of bags with them. So I'm queuing up for a ticket for the train, and the next minute I'm in this cubicle sitting on a toilet with a guitar playing *Bittersweet Symphony*. But on my right, Vernon Kay is presenting this Chinese game show, torturing this fella, with video static over everything."

"Hahahahaha."

"But Vernon Kay is dead, and somehow he's uploaded his consciousness into this game show. And I'm meant to be playing *Bittersweet Symphony* on the toilet as part of it. I can see my legs on a huge TV screen in the studio on my right. Then beyond that, the train station from earlier."

"I wonder what happened to the fella who was being tortured?"

"I can't decide which one was the dream within the dream within the dream."

"I carry that type of dream around with me all day. Impossible to shake."

"Anyway, I'm in Molloy's bedroom then and the actor who plays Truman Capote appears, to explain that it was all down to him fucking with some space continuum or other. That's why I was on the Chinese game show. Total nonsense, like."

The Liverpool Olympia was built in 1905 as a variety theatre and indoor circus. It lies in the Everton district of the city, about five minutes drive out of the centre, almost next door to the infamous Grafton nightclub and down the road from the derelict buildings where the Red Triangle karate group used to train.

These days, it's used mostly as a boxing, wrestling or mixed martial arts venue. It's huge, and tonight is a sell-out.

We enter the venue through a pair of huge retracting doors at the back. The scale of the place is overwhelming. I speak to Ben, a monitor engineer who came up with us in the early days. He says: "Have you seen the circular pit where they used to walk the elephants? It's behind a pair of locked doors in the basement. You can ask someone to open it up for you."

Post-gig, I wander around the catacombs in a daze, stopping every ten seconds or so to say hello to people I know, family, and people who've travelled from abroad to see us.

I have to shoot off soon after because I'm DJing in Duffy's brother's new place on Hardman Street, where I'll stay until the streets are bathed in a Hammer Horror mist that creeps in from the river.

Liverpool, 10/12/16

MYSTERY HOUSE/ NORWICH

In a hotel called The Great George, somewhere off a side road on the way out of Norwich, we're stood in a reception area waiting to be checked in. It's 2am. and the place smells like the communal TV room of an old people's home, just after they've eaten dinner.

We're stood there next to a giant fibreglass reindeer and this huge polar bear mannequin that has patches of its skin missing, as if it's contracted some kind of toxic mange. Below a huge wreath on the back wall, there is an ornate cuckoo clock. The ticking of its second hand is all we can hear while the receptionist checks us in.

Outside, a mist has descended and everything looks as if we've walked into a scene from *Poirot*.

Through a window, Duffy points out an outdoor sign that says 'THE NORWICH ROTARY CLUB MEET HERE EVERY TUESDAY', which he says, "sounds like some sort of threat. Don't hang around here on that day. They'll have you fucking lynched."

Norwich, 13/12/16

BRISTOL

Man Dressed As Batman Chases 'Killer Clowns' In Cumbria - The Daily Telegraph

I'm standing on the fourth floor of the Hampton By Hilton hotel, looking down at a couple of high street comic stores that I'm thinking I could finish the last of my Christmas shopping in.

The rest of the band have gone to the St Nicholas Market near here, but I'm feeling like I could do without the hike. I climb back into bed and listen to Cass McComb's *Mangy Love* on my phone after reading about it in a magazine I bought in a servo.

Eventually a restless feeling gets the better of me and I throw some clothes on and get out.

I go to a comic shop called Excelsior! Comics, and buy a graphic novel called *East Of West*. James recommended it earlier in the day. It's set on a post-apocalyptic planet, and is one of the best recent graphic novel series, I'm told.

I walk through town and enter the St Nicholas Market. At first, it looks like some strange emporium that you'd see at the beginning of a film like *Indiana Jones,* at the top of a mountain range in Tibet somewhere. The market itself is indoors, and you're immediately hit by the smell of exotic herbs, spices and cooking food. I almost expect a herd of goats to come milling past. I mooch about in a record shop called Payback for a while, before meeting up with James, Ian and Jack in a café.

In 2005, the band went to Bristol for an early demo session that would go on to constitute a chunk of the *Invisible Invasion* album. We travelled down to Geoff Barrow of Portishead's studio, after Alan Wills suggested we go outside the confines of the county to record a new LP.

We worked in the small second floor studio there, in a quiet industrial unit on a council estate next to a supermarket. It was us, Geoff and Adrian Utley, and they'd tell us about those early days in Bristol; the importance of bands like Smith & Mighty, the formation of The Wild Bunch, how Geoff himself began young, as a studio tape-op, chain-smoking nervously through sessions.

Between takes, we'd kick a ball around outside, and later go down and explore the record shops of Bristol, the steep road with the clothes stores and basement restaurants, and you could find dub and northern soul and rare hip hop records there more readily than most cities I'd been in.

Geoff's thing was that music was about attitude more than anything else, and that it was something criminally missing from the modern landscape. You can hear it in the production of that album. It doesn't compromise in any way. It turned out a strange, almost unfinished thing that reflected the thread of instability that ran through the band around that time, but one that remains a favourite.

Before tonight's gig, we go to a small Italian restaurant that's decked out like a Christmas grotto. It's just the band, and it strikes me that there are few moments during a tour where we find ourselves exclusively in the company of each other. We begin to make plans for next year; recording new songs, publishing this tour diary, organising another exhibition of the album artwork.

Then it's decided that we might go and watch Status Quo in Liverpool the day before Christmas Eve. As sort of a 'work night out'. Before I know it, tickets are booked.

Post-gig, Geoff comes backstage and says he's so bladdered he can't drink another beer. He has a can of coke instead. He's been out at the Invada Records Christmas party since 1 o'clock this afternoon, and has "taken the knock".

We talk about the recent European tour Geoff has been on with his band, BEAK>, which saw him putting his back out in the second day while throwing up in a motorway layby somewhere in Belgium. After that, we get to talking about movie soundtracks and production.

At one point, Geoff says:

"You should have always produced yourselves anyway."

"We probably will now."

"Should have started ages ago I reckon."

"Yeah. But we've picked up some good stuff off the people we've worked with. There are tricks to production."

"What, like charging loads of money for doing shit that the band can do better themselves?"

"S'pose."

Bristol, 15/12/16

NETWORK

There is a network of people who anchor me down when I start drifting away from the earth. Like the inflatable pig on the cover of Pink Floyd's *Animals* album that broke from its mooring at Battersea Power Station. The anchoring comes in the form of text messages, and pierce through the skin like darts of truth. There are seven people in the network:

One believes she can change the weather with her thoughts.
One is a recorder of dreams.
One is a blood relative.
Another is a blood relative.
One lost his shoe in the Kop end.
One is a member of a Birkenhead snooker hall.
One has worn Adidas Samba since 1976.
One brought me into this world.

I'm sitting here at a table in a market in Bristol waiting for *any one of them* to get in touch.

St Nicholas Market, Bristol, 15/12/16

MOLLOY PLAYLIST/ LONDON ROUTE

The Creation – *Making Time*
Charlie Feathers – *Can't Hardly Stand It*
The Monks – *I Hate You*
The Stooges – *Search and Destroy*
Black Sabbath – *Children Of The Grave*
Shocking Blue – *Send Me A Postcard*
The Sonics – *The Witch*
The White Stripes – *Seven Nation Army*
The Who – *Heaven And Hell*
The Kinks – *I'm Not Like Everybody Else*

Motorway, 16/12/16

LONDON

Early wake and meet in the hotel canteen for a breakfast buffet that promises “black pudding tractor wheels” and “big beanz”. The black puddings look evil, hubcaps of charcoal that stare back from the warming trays like possessed hockey pucks.

Half an hour later, as we make our way toward the motorway, we decide to listen to a Hawkwind compilation to fire us up for tonight’s gig in the capital:

‘*It’s a cerebral vibrator/ those energy stimulators/ just turn your eyeballs into craters/ but an orgone accumulator/ is a superman creator.’*

By the time we reach the Shepherd’s Bush Empire, we’re conducting a high voltage of nervous energy, and we pose excitedly for photographs under the holy glow of the bright marquee.

I’m soundchecking now in the main hall of the Empire building. High up, beyond a beautiful oyster shell-shaped ceiling arc, there is a perfect, bright moon, hovering weightlessly in the black sky. I look up and try to picture the faces of all the men who ever walked on its surface. I memorised them once, but they’ve disappeared now. Vanished from memory.

We eat a sort of last supper together in an amazing Turkish restaurant around the corner from the venue. We figure it’ll be the final meal before the madness of Manchester ensues tomorrow, where a sea of friends and family will descend on the Oxford Road Academy building, and we’ll inevitably split into separate factions.

Back in the dressing room, I’m leafing through a book of photographs called *American Motel Signs 1982-2008.* Somebody plays *Catch A Fire* on the stereo and it puts everyone in a good mood for the show.

A photographer we know, John Badham appears in the pit just before we go on. During the gig, he’s taking pictures at a furious rate, beads of sweat pouring down his face. He’s wearing a green Christmas jumper with a huge impression of Morrissey’s face knitted into the chest. It grabs my attention, even as I’m playing.

Behind Badham, in the front row, I can see a tall blonde girl dancing. She’s throwing the kind of shapes that you might see on old concert footage of space rock bands like Faust or Brainticket. Her eyes are as wide as frisbees, drinking in the spectrum of colour on the screen behind us.

We play a weighty, evil version of *Million Eyes* tonight. We've really gotten to grips with the dynamics of the song. As expected, *I Remember When* and *Bill McCai* go down well and set the newer, heavier songs up nicely.

About three minutes after we've come off stage, a slew of people heave up the stairwell and into the dressing room. There are champagne bottles being popped, people stood on tables, in the corridors, in the toilets. I can't see more than three yards in front of me because of the smoke.

Badham shows with the girl who was dancing at the front earlier. As I'm signing a bunch of album sleeves, she strikes up a conversation with Molloy, who's sat on the couch next to me. She begins it like this.

"You know Jaffa Cakes contain absolutely no orange?"

"I wasn't aware, no."

"None, not a bit."

"I'll bear that in mind."

"I was at your Liverpool show you know?"

"Oh, did you enjoy it then?"

"I had a panic attack in the front row and had to be stretchered out. But you sounded great from the ambulance."

London, 16/12/16

MANCHESTER

I sleep a deep sleep all the way down the motorway. A deeper sleep than I've slept all year, in fact. It's weird. I don't remember opening my eyes once between London and Manchester. I dream heavily and when I wake it feels like I've been unconscious for days. The final show of the year is passing by like a fading apparition.

We eat in a small kebab house next to the venue called Abdul Hadi, which serves up great chicken Kati rolls. As we're ordering, a group of men traipse in and I recognise one of them as James Hunter, the soul singer. We get talking and I tell him that we'd not long been listening to his album *People Gonna Talk*, and how it soundtracked a small period in the band's life. Hunter explains that the band are fresh back from America with a new album and are playing the same building as us tonight, but in a different room.

"Sometimes the planets align like that," he says. "And, oh, have you got a number for doo-dah by the way?"

The evening show is almost too much to take in. It's the end of the tour, the end of the year, and everything is tinged with conflicting emotions; relief and melancholy mixed together.

Big John is staying over in Manchester tonight, and so the remaining five of us jump in a hackney and pile all of our bags into the front, back, and onto our knees.

It's a tight squeeze and a long journey of swigging from open wine bottles and fumbling under seats for stray cans of dressing room lager. By the time we reach Marvin Powell's flat, where he and The Sundowners are having an all-nighter, I have to be woken by everyone laughing and banging the back window, as I'm nearly driven away in the dark cab.

Manchester, 17/12/16

THE LONG AND WINDING ROAD

Coming back from tour, no matter where from, sees us follow the same route home. I can't explain why. Grinding up the motorway, we pass a sign for Knowsley and then glide under a flyover that still has a Capital Of Culture '08 logo beamed against its grey concrete.

We almost always drop a monitor engineer or a guitar tech off at The Rocket pub, then grind into town, half-asleep as the city's underbelly wakes from its slumber.

Another drop-off might see us whizz past Seaforth and through Bootle, the container cranes silhouetted and skeletal, new beacons of hope for the haunted docks.

Into the city then, past the Albert Dock and the three graces, the Liver Building's bright Halloween orange clock face taking on some extra potency, an increased gothic drama in the early hours.

About then, I begin to think of Alan Wills in the old days, full of fevered monologues, and then the skilled pragmatism of Ian Broudie, figureheads that helped shape us before we moved back over the water to our hometown.

And I'm always glad to be home, or near home by this point, thankful that I live far away enough from the city not to be swallowed by it, but close enough to witness its bright luminosity, to feel its warmth.

We've burned through enough backwoods and retail-park cities in the US and across Europe to know that most places are ghost towns. Void of ideas, or the concept of ideas, anyway. Complete soul-holes. You'll know where I mean if you've ever been to one. A lot of out-of-city towns seem like a purgatory. I know where I live still has the roar of blood in its veins. Other places aren't so lucky.

Once, during a session from *The Curse Of Love* period, we decided, last-minute, to go to Blackpool the following day. Steve Adge was roped in to drive us, and we stopped off at 11am to buy crates of cider. The trip was organised through nothing else but sheer boredom.

You drop anchor in Blackpool and instantly feel as if you entered some skewed time-warp, some Victorian-era merged with the 70s. The chip shops and faded tea rooms. The horse-drawn carriage and its weary gait up and down the promenade. Candy floss girls who stare out from bright rock shop counters, braiding their own hair.

Only being an hour away, we bobbed into Blackpool by midday, to find that the pleasure beach was shut, completely deserted in the February mist. The whole fair was closed. So we mooched around the arcades all day, swigging Stella, trying to find a point to it all. We listened to The Smiths on the way up, the *Hatful Of Hollow* album. I couldn't get it out of my head. *The rain falls hard on a humdrum town.*

Blackpool itself has its own ghosts, an end-of-the-world desolation that haunts most of the old English seaside resorts. As if the modern world is exerting some mean cover up, consigning them to history like some shameful affair.

On returning, I look at Liverpool and drink it in. The beautiful blinking night cranes. The tall silhouettes and sleeping silver river. Even by night, it's impossible to deny that the city is alive. It always will be. Along with Manchester, which has its own weighty pulse, the two cities dominate the North West like a pair of dark stars.

Where I live, over the river is separate; has its own rules, its own ways. The city looks back like some overbearing sibling. But the draw is there, the magnetic pull. As we arrive home in the early hours, back from some festival in Taunton or Kent, Glasgow or Stafford, we transcend the city and leave it again, dip through the Kingsway tunnel as if some gateway to the afterlife. It's here I usually wonder if those nights travelling down long strips of empty motorway were nothing more than some kind of extended hallucination.

NOBODY SPEAK

And that's how it usually ends. Wide awake,
ghosting under the river.